Made-Up

Made-Up

a true story of beauty culture under late capitalism

DAPHNÉ B.

translated by ALEX MANLEY

COACH HOUSE BOOKS, TORONTO

First English-language edition. Originally published as *Maquillée* by Les Éditions Marchand de feuilles, 2020.

Canada Council for the Arts | Conseil des Arts du Canada | ONTARIO ARTS COUNCIL CONSEIL DES ARTS DE L'ONTARIO an Ontario government agency un organisme du gouvernement de l'Ontario | Canada

Coach House Books acknowledges the financial support of the Government of Canada. We are also grateful for generous assistance for our publishing program from the Canada Council for the Arts and the Ontario Arts Council. Coach House Books also acknowledges the support of the Government of Canada through the Canada Book Fund.

LIBRARY AND ARCHIVES CANADA CATALOGUING IN PUBLICATION

Title: Made-up : a true story of beauty culture under late capitalism / Daphné B. ; translated by Alex Manley.
Other titles: Maquillée. English
Names: B., Daphné, author. | Manley, Alex (Poet), translator.
Identifiers: Canadiana (print) 20210291001 | Canadiana (ebook) 2021029101X | ISBN 9781552454299 (softcover) | ISBN 9781770566828 (EPUB) | ISBN 9781770566835 (PDF)
Subjects: LCSH: Cosmetics. | LCSH: Beauty, Personal. | LCGFT: Essays. | LCGFT: Prose poems.
Classification: LCC PS8603.A1 M3713 2021 | DDC C843/.6—dc23

Made-Up is available as an ebook: ISBN 978 1 77056 682 8 (EPUB); 978 1 77056 683 5 (PDF)

not just wellness
prettiness
niceness
a highlight on the tip of your nose
on cupid's bow
on the cheeks

– Maude Veilleux,
from *Une sorte de lumière spéciale*

Schmoney.

The anarchist pop star had a baby with the son of a billionaire. It's a little green-grey wad of cash and guns. Proof, for those who needed it, that she hadn't really meant the things she'd said.[1, 2, 3]

I think about the pop star's baby with the billion-heir often.

I think about it, that little green-grey wad, the amalgamation of cash, of guns – about that colour at the intersection of wealth and violence, infinitely interlacing strands of the same fabric all come together. I try to understand the colour, to put the complexity of it into words. The green-grey wad, as murky as dirty water. Opaque, which works for it. That wad would love to cover up the banality of the truth: wealth comes from the barrel of a gun.

A wad isn't just a crumpled-up thing – it's also a stack of bills. Opulence, you see, presupposes scarcity – it blooms brightest in the garden of other people's misery. That intimate relationship between money and violence. This baby was born a gunslinger.

The baby that Anne Boyer describes isn't actually grey. More greyish. Nor is it green – more greenish. In fact, if you look closely, it's an ever-shifting, mutable hue. Hence the 'ish'es. It's forever on the doorstep of another shade, metamorphosing, a decomposing organ. Did you know that a

1. TRANS. NOTE: Throughout the text, Daphné weaves a web of poetic references that appear and disappear without warning. The authors of these texts will appear as footnotes. Academic citations are introduced more formally within the text.

2. Anne Boyer, 'No World But the World,' *Garments Against Women* (Boise: Ahsahta Press, 2015), 18. A French-to-English translation via Daphné B.'s version; the original reads: 'The anarchist pop star had a baby with the billionaire's son. It's a green gray blur of guns and money. It was proof for those who needed it that she didn't really mean what she said.'

3. TRANS. NOTE: Daphné's original translation of Boyer's lines here is more of an adaptation, and her translation of 'blur' as 'motton' – and then weaving the term *motton* in later – didn't allow for a straightforward use of the original. Thus, this text uses a translation of a translation.

dead person's kidney goes from brown to black? The trachea, which starts out white, becomes red, before landing on olive-ish. Colour is movement – it traps us in the steps of a dance, one that no one is allowed to sit out.

For a long time, I believed that poetry was prophecy, that it could tell us about the future: coming deaths, impending technological breakthroughs, new elements pulling up chairs at the periodic table. But that's not quite it. Rather, the images in poems are ones that necessitate – that must continue to necessitate – new words entirely. In which case, poetry isn't prophecy but, rather, outside of time entirely. 'It's not a question of what happens – poetry is outside of time. In fact, 'there's a much greater likelihood that poetry happens to you, while many things that may seem more important than poetry won't.'[4] That's Jean Cocteau, speaking to the year 2000 in a YouTube video. In short, poetry isn't current events – but nothing happens without it.

Did Anne Boyer know that the baby at the intersection of art and commerce she was writing about would one day be born, that, three years after her book came out, that little green-grey thing she'd imagined would be real-live tabloid fodder?

After all, the poet isn't an inventor. She's simply describing what's already there. Because what is reality, like the green-grey baby, *except proof for those who needed it?*

In May 2018, the Canadian singer Grimes, self-proclaimed anti-imperialist, drew back the curtains on her new relationship with billionaire businessman Elon Musk, the twenty-third richest person in the United States. Before the great reveal, of course, she made sure to wipe the word *anti-imperialist* from her Twitter bio. A bit of an awkward signifier, after all, for someone who's dating a guy publicly committed to colonizing Mars.

I knew Grimes as the princess of Montreal's underground scene, ruler over dusty lofts and the chemicals we use to loosen

4. 'Jean Cocteau s'adress a l'an 2000,' viewable at: https://www.youtube.com/watch?v=3-t1Wo8JEdQ. My translation; original quotes: 'Elle ne correspond pas à ce qui se passe; elle est inactuelle;' 'Il y a quelques chances pour qu'elle vous arrive, alors que beaucoup de choses qui semblent plus importantes ne vous arrivent pas.'

up. She had greenish, blackish, pinkish hair; she locked herself in studios for days on end, without eating or sleeping, birthing new albums of experimental music. A cyborg, pop and metallic, bathed in clouds of shimmering soot, wielding a sword and speaking in snake-like tongues. Her songs sounded like a high kicking in, like the speed with which we came down.

I bring her up because we went to the same university, Grimes and I, because she was the friend of one friend of mine, and the lover of another. At one point, long before she was going out with one of the world's most powerful men, before she was promoting her music on billboards that blared that global warming was a good thing, I used to feel a kinship with her. One of my exes told me about the parties she used to throw – her dingy apartment, the grunge in her bathtub, a blackish juice. *It was grimy*, he said. It was Grimes. Of course, that dinginess, that grunginess, that griminess isn't new to me – it haunts just about every affordable apartment in Montreal. Even as I write this, there are rivulets of rain coming through the ceiling.

When news of Grimes and Musk's itemhood broke, I was seeing a well-known sociologist. Thirtysomething, shaven-headed, rebel without a clue. The kind of socialist who can't feel anything when he's wearing a condom, you know the type. So radical, with his all-black outfits, his various pins and patches. He lived in Los Angeles, worked for a publicly traded company, and drove a Beemer. I remember how shocked he seemed when we discussed his beloved singer's dirty laundry. A capitalist Grimes? It was more than he could take. He was dejected, practically disgusted. But I think maybe he was most disgusted by the Grimes he felt beating inside his own rib cage.

There's nothing more repulsive than seeing your own weaknesses in another. That's why we're so revolted by corpses – we see in them our own fate. One day, that'll be us:

'A disgusting mess whose shame our loved ones will have to cover up from survivors,' as Bataille puts it.[5] To be disgusted is to be nauseated – a desperate spasm, an attempt to distance the self from the self.

What had Grimes done, in shacking up with Mr. Imperialist, if not render visible the inherent contradictions of the twenty-first century, the ones constantly threatening to tear us all limb from limb? Everything is both itself and its own opposite. Even the desires that drive me are contradictory ones. I both love and hate the idea of the world ending. In fact, I often catch myself awaiting the apocalypse, even opening the door for it a notch. I accept it as the 'natural' conclusion of the elastic experience of existence – one that's already pulled taut and ready to snap.

Deep in the heart of my apartment, alone in a global pandemic, I won't think about anything, except maybe buying myself a grapefruit-scented candle online. I'll want my world to at least smell nice while it's ending. I'll learn how to dye my hair from YouTube videos. I'll take the online test that lets you know how many Earths we'd need if everyone had the same patterns of consumption as I do. It'll tell me: 3.6 Earths. I'll apologize for that.

Hell, I apologize for everything. Sometimes even for apologizing. I've got 3.6 Earths in my gut and another one stuck in my throat. Some days, I beg for the end of the world the way Catholics ask for forgiveness. It's soothing, in a way, to imagine my own end.

I think about my L.A. sociologist. I wonder whether he really thinks he can escape from the dissonance this century has trapped us all in.

If so, then pray for me, Saint Sociologist.

5. Georges Bataille, 'La Mort,' *L'Histoire de l'érotisme* (Montréal: Gallimard, 1976), 79. My translation. The original: 'Ignominieuse pourriture dont nos proches auront le soin de dérober la honte à la vue des survivants.'

Made-up, ensconced in my bed, and listening to a song about money, I'm filling my Sephora cart to the brim: two iridescent eyeshadow palettes, an eyeliner, and a bottle of retinol. With a click of the mouse, a third of a month's rent goes up in smoke. I just made a star go nova, ended a royal line of butterflies, burned a field of clover to ashes. Soon, a truck will come to my door, bearing a little box.

I'm not doing anything to slow the apocalypse's approach. No, for four hours now, I've been superglued to my computer screen. The Conspiracy palette – an eyeshadow collaboration between the American YouTubers Jeffree Star and Shane Dawson[6] – just dropped. Two minutes before its launch, the sheer volume of would-be purchasers crashed Shopify, the e-commerce platform the duo were using. 'Y'all broke the internet!' Star hastens to explain to his frustrated fans as they try in vain to acquire a Conspiracy of their own.

This digital crash, however, wasn't just a rogue wave. Between them, Star and Dawson have over 39 million YouTube subscribers,[7] a literal human tsunami. While Shopify works hard to rebirth the e-store from its ashes to permit the mechanisms of capitalism to resume their functioning, the duo's feverish fans rush to Twitter. One of them posts a video of herself in the hospital, pushing her IV drip over to the nearest window, phone in hand, the better to capture the nearest signal. She doesn't want to lose her place in the digital waiting room: 'On my way to the window trying to get some signal so i can hopefully get the #ShaneDawsonXJeffreeStar #Conspiracy-Palette 👀 since I wasn't able to leave the hospital and go to a Morphe store 😭 '

Everyone seems touched by this act of sincere devotion – myself included. Dawson himself tears up. Or rather, I should

6. TRANS. NOTE: Since this was written, both have been dogged by serious allegations of past racism.

7. As of November 2019.

say, Dawson himself tweets out a handful of crying emojis. In the conference room from which the launch is being broadcast, someone suggests to the duo of the hour that they might have more clout than the president. And it might just be true – at this exact moment, they're exerting a kind of gravitational pull on millions of people around the world. Like two celestial bodies, Shane and Jeffree are subtly shifting the trajectory of my orbit – mine and that of so many others. The digital waiting room counts over 2.5 million anxious buyers, and on some level, we are all the girl in the hospital, pushing her IV drip to the window, refreshing her screen. Four hours later – before I get a chance to buy one for myself – just over a million Conspiracy palettes have flown off the pixelated shelves.[8] The collection is sold out. It's a historic moment for the beauty industry.

I'm not in L.A., nor am I going out with the CEO of Tesla Motors. I've never even released an album. Still, how can I draw a neat dividing line between myself and our favourite contradictory pop star, the girl 'who doesn't really mean the things she says,' if I just made a day go up in smoke fantasizing about a makeup palette? And it wasn't the first time that's happened, either. I'm a feminist, a poet, and a translator. I try to root out the forces of capitalism, sexism, racism, and colonialism that have taken up refuge inside me. And even though I give myself permission to speak loudly, to push back against the overconfident men, broadcasting live from state radio, I myself am not immune to the forces that I decry. I'm embarrassed to be a consumer, to use up the wick of my life a few hours at a time at the altar of these websites, so adept at engaging with my inexhaustible desires. My sex drive might wax and wane, but I'm always hungry for product. It could be anything: a new eyeshadow, a nice pair of shoes, a bottle of orange wine. A Pogo made of seal meat. Some days, I can't

8. In an Instagram story, Star claimed that they'd sold 1.1 million units.

even convince myself the inertia of this consumerism is a form of self-care. I think about my privilege. I think about the blood on my butter-soft hands. But shame is a poor kind of brake mechanism.

When I was living in Taipei, an old lady on my street sold sweet potatoes cooked over charcoal. I always hurried past her stall. I didn't sell sweet potatoes. I knew I'd never have to sell sweet potatoes in my life. Instead I'd slip away to jog the length of a river full of dirty water, praying it would give me a perfectly sculpted ass. Those days, I managed to sneak out of my torpor to chain-smoke on my balcony. I was finding ecstasy in self-destruction. It seemed like a form of salvation – it was nice to believe that, killing myself little by little, I was slowly repenting for the sin of my existence. 'Even if there's nothing wrong with shame when it humbles us,'[9] when it does, I can feel the greenish-greyish baby, that wad of cash and guns, kicking inside my stomach.

Like a dewdrop hanging from a thread of a complex and flexible web, I'm not outside the green-grey of capital; I'm caught up in the shroud of its vibrations. A spiderweb, I read on Wikipedia, is a type of trap. Some days, I'm the prism the sun shines through: it's me making the system shimmer. Made-up, besequined, McDonaldized – I am the rain that turns the trap crystalline.

Some days, I wish I could stop sweeping my shame under this rug of cigarette ash and suicidal ideation. I wish I could listen to it. Learn from it.

9. Nicholas Dawson, *Désormais, ma demeure* (Triptyque, 2020), 156. Translation my own.

I'm swimming in a sea of plenty, a fertile crescent of forbidden fruit. I'm clicking on products. Shopping in the void. I make myself a sugar-baby profile on SeekingArrangement.com and dare to fantasize about being paid for that which I've always given away for free. Five hundred bucks to talk to me, to kiss me, to fuck me. Come to me, I think, to the sugar daddies of the world; come to me, PapaLouisVuitton, Daddy's_Home, and InterstellarFox. I'm tracking the likes, the messages. I'm filtering these masked men – many of them older than my father – by annual income and net worth. As I walk along the street in Outremont, my eyes convert every older man I pass into a sugar daddy. Aren't they all just looking for a friend to play with, all benefits, no strings attached? Daddy will take care of you. They've probably figured out by now that women like me are emotional breakdowns waiting to happen, cursed with overactive imaginations of the heart. No drama, they say, and it feels like a pre-emptive strike.

The doorbell rings. My little box has come. I've found a purpose once again, a *raison d'être*: opening little boxes. It's like I've found a new religion: shrouds, cerements, intricate cases – the deluxe makeup I buy comes wrapped so lovingly you'd swear it was a holy relic. My Pat McGrath blushes come in little plastic baggies full of sequins, so when I tear them open, a rain of gold anoints my sheets. Bling bling – the kind I can afford, anyway. Whether it's Chanel, YSL, Marc Jacobs, or Armani, cosmetics and perfumes have always functioned as metaphors for a still greater luxury. By making the haute couture houses they represent a little bit more attainable, they create an illusion – a sort of ghost wealth, accessible to everyone.

In order to fit in with the upper crust, one sometimes needs to alter one's identity. I read that Florence Nightingale Graham rechristened herself Elizabeth Arden in order to open her own salon in 1910. She used that name to build her cosmetics empire, and a woman who started out a Canadian nurse, a simple farmer's daughter, ended up representing the very opulence that she had once sought to recreate. Fake it 'til you make it, as they say. Anyway, her tombstone reads Elizabeth, not Florence.

On SeekingArrangement, I rechristen myself poetbaby. I wonder if any of the fifteen daddies who've recently visited my profile can tell that I'm not a *real* sugar baby. My eyes betray my age; I've got bruises and stray hairs, cells considering going cancerous. All I want to do is hurt these men and then whisper in their ears: '*No drama.*'

On second thought, the greenish-greyish baby of capitalism might be verdigris instead – the colour that blossoms on copper monuments as they corrode.

It's the green of statues and government buildings, the official symbol of every roof with a long and storied heritage, Montreal's city hall, the *hôtel de ville*. It's everyone who ever told me that I'd understand when I was older, when I had kids of my own. It's my mother calling me a slut. It's the police and the mayor hiking public transit fees. It's Lady Liberty lighting up the world from her perch off the southern tip of Manhattan.

This colour, verdigris, welds itself to the power of the state, to the logics of surveillance, to the mechanisms of control. Watch as the copper oxidizes, and the buildings, barracks, pyramids erected in the gold rush of colonization cover themselves up with a literal patina of respectability. Listen as the copper trembles in the wind like blood-red leaves turned back to green. It's a process of chemical degradation, but ironically, the further it erodes, the more its very hue demands our respect and obedience.

My great-grandfather used to work in a copper mine, extracting that precious colour with the sweat of his brow. Then, December 26, 1941, he fell 1,300 feet to the bottom of the No. 4 well in the Noranda mine. My grandmother, Ghislaine, was just eighteen months old.

> *When Johnson and Blais each had one foot in the elevator and one foot on the ground of the 1200 level, the winch operator got the signal to bring the elevator back up. He had no idea that the signal had been given mistakenly; when the elevator began to rise, Johnson managed to get out, but Blais, caught off guard by the sudden movement, rose up with it until it reached the highest point of the shaft. From there he fell, likely unconscious, into the yawning hole.*

My great-grandfather didn't typically work the day after Christmas. He knew that hard-drinking miners, still hungover from their parties the night before, were much more likely to slip up and commit a fatal error. That year, he'd made an exception, though – he needed the money. The newspaper clipping that recounts the story of the accident describes his corpse as having been mangled beyond recognition.

> *As he fell, his body was torn up by the mine shaft's timbering. At the bottom of the well, all that was left of the unfortunate victim was a formless mass of flesh. It took several hours of painstaking work to round up all of his remains.*

The story of a person killed by the very workplace that exploited them is the story of the merger between human flesh and the cold, hard wad of cash and guns. It's a factoid, a news item that restarts the poem over and over, a text that's forever outside of time.

In the slim notebook where my great-grandmother told her life's story in forty pages of blue ink, the horror of her husband's death takes up just two sentences. It's important, she points out, to spare the children.

Today, all that's left of that mine is the Horne foundry, with its two chimneys that, year in and year out, cough tons and tons of arsenic, lead, and sulphur dioxide into the sky. According to my family in Abitibi, the air in Rouyn-Noranda has a distinct smell to it. Even a bite to it, a sort of grittiness.

I visit the region on my MacBook Air, through a dense forest of windows and tabs. 'By day, the sky is unbelievably blue; by night, occasionally, you get supernatural Northern Lights,' one tourism site claims. I read that particles of arsenic in the air increase the risk of lung cancer, and it's hard not to think of the spherical little tumour that killed my grandmother. 'It's the kind of cancer we only see in Vietnam vets,' her doctor told us. I click on another article, one about the foundry. It's described as 'the beating heart of Rouyn-Noranda's economy.' The light from my screen bleeds blue.

I keep scrolling. *Suivant,* next. I download PDFs, photos of necrotized gooseberry bushes, ash trees, poplars. I listen to Raôul Duguay on Spotify. In his song 'La bitt à Tibi,' he mentions the Harmonica River, but it's nowhere to be found on Google Maps. I wish I could go float down it, fish for a bit, maybe take a little nap in the riverbed, and rest up for a century or so.

In 2012, a writer known only as Beach Sloth printed T-shirts that said 'I want to YouTube down the rivers of America,' which he sold on his website alongside coffee mugs bearing the same phrase. Today, the site is under construction, and his career seems to have fallen down the same hole that claimed the rest of Alt Lit,[10] the online writing community he was once a part of.

At the time, I wore that shirt everywhere – to bed, to school – while I filled my life to the brim with the busywork of watching makeup videos online. I was YouTubing down the rivers of my waking life, even my nights, not really sure what it was I was looking for. Getting drunk on the voices of beautiful anonymous women as they broke down everything I needed to know about every conceivable makeup product. They talked to me about shine, about smell; about pigments and texture. I followed makeup reviews like my ancestors might have followed the North Star. I was – and am – always hungry for more advice, regardless of whether I bought anything afterward. Their voices soothed me when my throat wanted to clench up. Their voices were terra firma to step on. Sometimes, to feel at peace, all you need is for someone to tell you what to buy: This is the best powder. This, the shiniest lip gloss. This, the mattest, creamiest, most vibrant lipstick.

Like a knight of Arthurian legend, I was looking for the Holy Grail. In the coded language of beauty YouTubers, an HG is an irreplaceable, almost mythical product, one you'd choose over all the others. It's the logical end point of a capitalist quest, a perfect match, its discovery worth celebrating, a homecoming for the weary, errant consumer. In this game, we are all a prince who's been tasked with a sacred mission: to find the perfect product, that sacred merch, tailor-made just for us.

10. Alt Lit was an informal literary community that formed online around 2011. While the genre had little by way of governing aesthetic, alt lit writing was typically informed by social media and a DIY ethic. A few years in, however, rocked by multiple allegations of sexual misconduct and rape involving key members, the community largely dissolved.

My doorbell rings again. This time, a Chanel lipstick. It's a little box wrapped in a shroud inside a bag. Tearing through all this packaging, I feel like I'm digging a tunnel to the primordial centre of the earth's molten core. As I remove each successive layer, I get closer to the tube; I feel the beating of its tell-tale heart, the many layers between us only stoking my excitement. Lust swells in the presence of the unattainable. 'Desire is about vanishing. You dream of a bowl of cherries and next day receive a letter written in red juice.'[11] We always want the ones we can't have, the hearts that beat in other directions. I'm on YouTube again, or else reading letters dripping with red.

Hi Daphné, yes, I'm sorry
I wish.
But I have
I hope you
be happy
be happy and well

I am happy. I am well. I'm getting drunk on unboxing videos, the meticulous mise en scènes of hands uncovering all kinds of products. I watch them, buzzed off the crinkling of paper, the scratching of acrylic nails against the hardness of chic boxes. It's consumption by proxy, an anesthetic pleasure. It doesn't matter whether the hands are breaking open a Kinder egg or unfurling the strap of a Rolex – what I find soothing is watching a product disrobe. Unboxings undress the inorganic; they're home videos of a striptease of consumption at the lip of true ownership. When I watch them, it feels like the hands onscreen are my hands – that I'm the one tearing away the wrapping, ripping open the boxes. I get a little taste of the mercurial pleasure of acquisition –

11. Anne Carson, *Norma Jeane Baker of Troy* (London: Oberon Books, 2019), 22.

imagining myself taking the object out of its box, holding it in my hands like a bluebird. One of my favourite makeup gurus often uploads videos where she does just that: unboxes PR packages, those promo swag bags that the big cosmetics companies send her every day. Today, she selects a handful of pieces to give away to her fans. 'I'm in the phase of Marie Kondo-ing the crap out of my life. I want this to bring someone else joy,' she says. That's the crux – it's joy that we're unwrapping, unboxing, and appraising. It's joy that I want to hold in my hands.

The video ends, and I watch my happiness fly off. At least I didn't spend a month's rent – just a few minutes of my time. I watch YouTube glide my raft on over to the next video.

On one of my YouTube meanderings, I came across a woman from Massachusetts named Makeup Kristi. In one of her videos, she tries out a sort of dirty emerald eyeshadow, its hue calling immediately to mind the one Anne Boyer described in her poem. It's thanks to Makeup Kristi, then, that I know the real name for the mutant colour of the greenish-greyish baby that the anarchist pop star had with the man who has too much money. The colour is called schmoney.

On the website for Estate Cosmetics, a Montreal-based company, I discover that Schmoney is a WTF-free eyeshadow – *that means no parabens, no phthalates, no animal cruelty. Like WTF, who needs that anyway?*, the site explains. The endless list of things their products *don't* contain performs the same function as those buzzy unboxing videos. By magicking away an unpleasant reality, the list is like a cradle. Comforting.

If Estate Cosmetics is making a big deal about its WTF-free products, it's a way to call attention to its own cleanliness of spirit. It's marking the bad thing as external, as foreign. Schmoney is baby angel emoji – innocent, wouldn't hurt a fly. Its enemies, meanwhile, are clearly designated. For five whole seconds, it feels like I know what to fear, what to avoid: sulfates, parabens, phthalates, formaldehyde. But that oversimplification elides the fact that violence comes in many forms, that the opalescence of our eyeshadows is based on a system that benefits but a select few. Unfortunately for Estate Cosmetics, makeup as a whole is far from being WTF-free.

On the product page, it says that Schmoney's intensity will last so long, it would have outlasted my last relationship. I try to swallow away the bad taste in my mouth. One user writes: *wierd green color. didnt go well with my skin.* I love it. The absurdity of it all can't even be spelled out.

Because it alters the face – the central nervous system of selfie culture – makeup might well be on its way to becoming the twenty-first century's defining product. If that's the case, Estate Cosmetics is right: Schmoney's vibrancy will outlive all my failed relationships. It'll outlast my own private catastrophes as well as those that stretch beyond me, those that rend the Earth apart, exposing its frail and beating core.

But Schmoney won't be satisfied to just keep on shining brightly throughout the years; the secret behind its luminescence is mica, a shiny mineral that can be found in just about every iridescent cosmetic product. Despite its star-spangled look, though, this rock comes from the earth; it's mined in India, often by children.

In a 2019 Refinery29 exposé, journalist Lexy Lebsack travels to the Indian state of Jharkhand to interview young, dust-covered miners.[12] They sport hollow stares, their clothes tarnished by a grime that's both glossy and matte. It's not YouTube videos that are sucking up these children's waking hours, it's work – seven days a week in cramped tunnels, passageways forever threatening to collapse. They're risking their lives to hunt for the stuff that will make me sparkle. It's a disgusting logic, and yet. 'It's the first time I've actually seen pretty dirt,' says Lebsack, staring at the dirt road leading to the mine's entrance. When I was younger, I thought of violence as a blood-and-viscera-stained affair, a chainsaw massacre. But sometimes violence is just a shimmering powder, an especially pretty kind of dirt.

Another YouTube video pops up. I watch someone make themselves up, and it's calming. There's something satisfying about this particular form of embellishment, the way it produces a concrete effect. Covering a face in foundation is

12. Refinery29, 'The Dark Secret Behind Your Favorite Beauty Products.' https://www.youtube.com/watch?v=IeR-h9C2fgc

like frosting a cake – the upshot is immediately visible, and easy to consume. The linear succession of steps in the transformation gives me a sense of closure, a half-hearted moment of pleasure. Still, it's better than nothing. For a second, caught between the lips of a beautiful YouTuber, I forget about the children stepping into the mouth of the mine.

The videos that dot the surface of YouTube are produced by people like me, those with the luxury of time on their hands. It's only natural, then, that the site fosters and promotes a particular privileged vision of the world, that of people with a certain baseline of free time. Time Is Money, the name of a rose-coloured eyeshadow with silver highlights, reminds me. Of course, the social web democratizes speech, in a way. Today's digital beauty culture is much more inclusive than the one I remember from my childhood, the one that made up the magazines my mother read: the models all too young, too skinny, too white. Today, those who used to be systematically erased from the glossy pages have gained much-needed visibility, and their outspokenness has given new life to the discourse surrounding the world of cosmetics. On YouTube, for example, beauty is no longer too young, too skinny, too white – now it's Black, it has acne, it's fat, disabled, and wrinkled, it comes in all genders and all ages. On the other hand, while the internet allows for members of otherwise under-represented communities to be seen, in order to be visible, first you must make your way up out of the mine shaft.

Conspiracy, too, features mica. In fact, it's at the top of the ingredient list on almost every eyeshadow in Dawson and Star's collection. Its omnipresence, however, doesn't seem to tarnish the palette's image – even before it went on sale, videos about it were topping the YouTube charts.

A mini-webseries, published on YouTube, documents the genesis of the palette. Each episode boasts tens of millions of views. Overwhelmed with excitement, one commenter even notes that they felt their heart fall into their butt. I get it – capitalism makes my heart beat faster, too. It's not just a system for producing goods and services, it must be said, but also a machine that spits out feelings, an assembly line of emotion.

For one month, I, like so many others, watched the webseries to follow the two business partners in their makeup adventure. I watched them christen their colours, watched them draw up the packaging and logos. I witnessed their tearful, anxious crises in a conference room in California. They spoke of money, percentages, net and gross profits, even of the $10 million they expected to make. This cash grab – cleverly sprinkled with slices of their lives, including a dying pet – distracted me from my own episodes, my own colours. 'Everyone's following this journey,' Star brags in one episode, and it's hard to argue with him.

I was more than a follower. I coloured outside the lines of my role; I overflowed its banks. My heart seized up when confronted with the pulse of an orange powder meant to resemble Cheeto dust. I wanted Star and Dawson to make $10 million; hell, I wanted them to make more. I thought that at the end of their palette's shimmery rainbow, I'd find something else, too – something like the ghost of my grandmother Ghislaine. She'd come to me in a vision, a cloud of curds and whey, and whisper a single word into my ear: *Tenderness*. My journey, too, could be a mythic story.

Journey, journey, journey, my CEGEP English teacher would say, swinging the word like a hammer. He was using 'The Journey of the Magi' – a Biblical poem by T. S. Eliot – to teach us about the essence of 'great literature.' I didn't understand its significance at the time, mistaking a journey I found boring for a simple trip. In the poem, three wise men cross the desert, half-crazed, following a star, missing the 'silken girls' they'd left back home. At the time, my professor said he could tell the difference between real poetry and fake poetry, between the good and the bad. His insistence on that particular journey, thus, was terrifying to me. What if, because I couldn't see what was so special about Eliot's tale, I was doomed to fakedom? At the time, I didn't yet know that the mere concept of fake poetry exists only to reassure those terrified that they, too, might be imposters.

In 'The Journey of the Magi,' the three wise men finally find Jesus in the straw, still red and slick with afterbirth. The speaker of the poem is shocked to discover that he's dying – *this Birth was/Hard and bitter agony for us, like Death, our death.* At the end of their trek, they found not just a newborn in the straw, but their own empty snakeskins, the past peeled away.

They'd changed.

Even the shortest of journeys means an inevitable surrender to change. Me, I'm living adventures from my bed, pressed up against my memory-foam pillow, guided by insomniac desire. I'm YouTubing my way through the rivers of night, following the Dawson and the Star, seeking out the birth that was foretold. I emerged from the descent without a mark on me, but full of a dawning appetite and an irrational attachment to an inanimate object: an eyeshadow palette. As the odyssey unspooled, I took the object – large, plastic – under my wing, like a small, yellowish animal with an injured paw. I cajoled it. At one point, it felt almost like I had played a role in its life.

When Shane decides to eliminate one jade-green eyeshadow from the palette-in-progress, it feels like an injury to a phantom limb. In my head, I name the fallen shade in honour of a friend. One YouTube commenter says, 'The unnamed green shade being taken out is so sad.' I mourn at the tomb of the unnamed colour. I'd never felt that way about a colour before, much less an eyeshadow. What's happening to me? I dove headfirst into a story, and now it feels like it's the story that's telling me.

A few weeks later, Dawson announces that he'll sell green hoodies to commemorate the 'unnamed green shade.' The colour's a little different from the one that got cut from the palette, but it remains essentially the same. Whether in hoodie or powder form, it's still a product.

I liked the palette so much, I wanted to own it, to put it on a leash and walk it. But while I was solemnly contemplating the mechanisms of the system, my scarf got caught in all the whirring pieces. I once had lofty plans, but here I am, dying, strangled. 'With anti-capitalists like me, capitalism is in no immediate danger,' writes the author Jacob Wren on Twitter.[13]

By so meticulously documenting the creation of their collection, Shane Dawson and Jeffree Star have inverted the traditional model of the product launch.[14] No longer are these things conceived in the dark – now, the whole process has become a spectacle: the ideation, the production, even the marketing itself is something that can be disseminated. The

13. From a tweet by Jacob Wren, November 12, 2019: https://twitter.com/EverySongIveEve/status/1194325574250090496?s=20.

14. This idea was put forth by Andrei Terbea in his video 'How the Conspiracy Palette SHOOK the Internet': https://www.youtube.com/watch?v=JHMJ-2Y7Xso, published November 9, 2019.

steps of the process, alchemized into reality TV, themselves become products. No detail is left unfilmed, from the phone calls with retailers to the exorbitant profit margins the two friends expect to make. There's an almost grotesque quality to their transparency, an honesty they turn around and profit off, because it forms the foundation of their brand image. They're long-time subscribers to the social media ethos, the one that calls for everyone to be authentic, natural, #nofilter. The two discuss their imminent cash grab over slushies and root beers, spontaneous, imperfect, human, and when the cameras pan over their untidy mansions, they're all too happy to slip in a nonchalant 'Excuse the mess.' A flower grows amidst the chaos, a poisoned intimacy, unidirectional.

I make my way back to SeekingArrangement. At what point does putting on makeup become pure procrastination? How many hours? How many clicks does it take to bring us a little closer to death? How many songs does it take to get us drunk?

I'm growing old online. I'm YouTubing my way down the rivers of America. The quote on my Beach Sloth shirt was also the title of his poetry collection, which came out in 2012. At the time, he announced the release of the book with the seriousness of Rafiki lifting baby Simba up before all the animals of the pridelands: 'Welcome to the first physical artifact of my online existence made by my very own hands. That used to be my body but I have merged to become one with the internet.'[15]

Me, too, I've merged to become one with the internet. It's a part of me, and of my books. My body is a mishmash of cells and pixels, passwords and likes. The old distinction – between 'online' and 'offline' – no longer exists. Today, there is no line at all; the world is no longer comprehensible outside the existence of the social web. I still remember, though, those childhood afternoons spent inventing different age/sex/locations for myself, playing fast and loose with my identity in chatrooms all over Québec – a man, a woman, a cat by turns. At the time, it made sense to describe the web as a 'virtual space' in literal terms, because it was still possible to transcend one's physical self. Today, the internet is criss-crossed by private interests that promote the usefulness of a stable identity, anchored in time, a single A/S/L. It makes sense – what is the value of data mined from fictional identities? Or shifting ones? In order to generate resellable information, you need solid ground – the substrate must be predictable.

15. Beach Sloth's website: https://www.beachsloth.com/i-want-to-youtube-down-the-rivers-of-america.html, consulted May 27, 2020.

Social media's ethos rejects anonymity in favour of a more authentic form of speech – or, at least, one that tries to pass itself off as such. The dream is for users to express themselves as themselves – spontaneously and under the banner of their real names, without wasting time conjuring up alternate selves. What luck for capital, then, that this leads to the generation of even more content! Spontaneity, after all, doesn't require anyone to carefully think through which things should be shared and which shouldn't.

As a corollary, there's an increasing demand for vulnerability. We're encouraged to transform our flaws, our cracks, our wounds into content, one FML and frowning emoji at a time. We like the pictures our friends post of their puffy, rubicund faces – they, too, are in the middle of an anxiety attack. These are our twenty-first-century sagas, our daily #MeToos. My favourite makeup gurus are always bursting into tears. They break down, get divorced, upload videos they claim contain the truth, the whole truth, nothing but the truth. The titles of their vlogs resemble nothing so much as admissions made to a therapist: *OPENING UP (vulnerable)* shouts one title posted by Jaclyn Hill, a beauty influencer and makeup artist hit by yet another scandal. I, too, am tearing myself apart, putting the abyss of my drunk texts, my spittle, my debts and demon mother on full display. By insisting on my own vulnerability, I'm feeding the corporations morsels of my self, the dark side of my moon clearly visible to their algorithms. They know I always have a tough time in February. By being forever vulnerable, though, I'm guaranteed to also be relatable – that is, to produce a discourse within which others will be able to see themselves. All of social media is just one big echoing web of 'me too's.

Each week, a new animal – ugly and feeble – rotates into the lead role of my conversations, becomes the Rosetta stone through which to read all my silly little social interactions. Often, it's a moving sight, the type of misshapen creature that we'd all love to save, to protect from the looming apocalypse. Eye-poppingly translucent, the word *vulnerable* practically tattooed on its skin. Whether it's a puppy with a tail growing out of its forehead, a microscopic tardigrade trundling through the void of space, or a naked mole rat, we consume the vulnerability of these creatures like we were eating a strawberry – the flesh tender, not too flavourful, just pink enough for us to feel touched, to feel like we, too, are a little bit pink. It's not a sense of caring that emerges from the encounters with these creatures so much as a sense of superiority. We perceive them as little monsters in need of our love. Confronted with the beast, we feel human – especially when it's a crooked, weak, and vulnerable little creature we feel like we could rescue. We must take the young sloth in our arms, help it to cross the busy street. Without us, it would surely be crushed by a passing car. On YouTube, someone's carrying one of these animals. They're so slow that algae grows over their fur like moss. I copy the link to the video and head over to Twitter. Send tweet.

The sloth represents a vulnerability that can be bought and copied – that can be printed on coffee mugs, soap dishes, shower curtains, T-shirts, even the foam art on your latte. Fragility can be claimed and worn like a shiny new button. The vulnerable things we consume calm us down, soothe us, as if stroking our senses of self. The image of the defenceless sloth gives us the illusion of having control over something. Even if you identify with the vulnerability it embodies, you feel like you can transcend it, could be the one who – high above the very real dangers the sloth faces

– can step in to prevent the worst from occurring, can protect it from death itself. To consume vulnerability like this is to fool ourselves into believing in our own power, our self-described invincibility.

Vulnerability is, in fact, a sign of life: a body capable of suffering, a body capable of love. And I fall for everything that crumples, breaks, or crumbles. It's always my lovers' imperfections that first seduced me. I believed I could crawl inside other people, like stuffing yourself into a secret hidey-hole. I wanted to descend through their fathomless depths. I once read in a short story that the temple of love is an underground cave into which seawater runs through a crack. And that the god of love isn't a being, but a sound – the eternal echo of the water's quick trickle and fall. The sound of the sea crashing against the walls of the abyss.[16]

My love life, then, was a long history of falling for crossed eyes, penguin waddles, sausage fingers, cauliflower ears. Discovering these secret anomalies in the bodies of those I loved, I was always a strange mix of proud and moved. That which is fragile has always seemed precious to me.

Internet celebrities are no strangers to this logic; they rarely hesitate to exhibit their imperfections. Their flaws and cracks, in fact, become the cornerstones of their images. Shane Dawson, for example, in keeping with his sympathetic former-fat-kid persona, spends his time drinking root beer and being kind.[17] A celebrity influencer and thirty-one-year-old millionaire, he still manages to clash visibly with the sheer flamboyance of Jeffree Star's aura: his legendary fake nails and multiplicity of wigs. In the Conspiracy webseries, Dawson seems to wear exclusively T-shirts covered in cat hair, a layer of feline grime that contrasts noticeably with the glitter and bling of the world he's now moving through. The pedestrian quality of his flaws humanizes him, brings him down to our level. Dawson has

16. From a short story by Antonio Tabucchi called 'Hesperides,' in *The Woman of Porto Pim*, translated from the Italian by Tim Parks (New York: Archipelago Books, 2013), 3–10.

17. TRANS. NOTE: Despite his staged 'kindness,' Dawson has a history of problematic and racist behaviour.

neither the royal airs nor the self-assurance of his business partner. Rather, he seems perpetually overwhelmed by emotions he cannot contain. They exude from his achingly sensitive body, forever on the verge of splitting apart, while the camera zooms in on his Balenciaga hoodie spotted with sweat, his ruddy face covered in breakouts. It's a painful spectacle – wouldn't it be easier to stop watching, to put down the rose-coloured glasses of him, rather than continue to feel our own fragility mirrored like this? Should we wrap him in a bear hug, blow-dry his tears, stifle his thousandth cry of 'omg,' break down and buy the palette? Dawson is flesh personified, at once tender and tenderized, a sort of memory-foam person his fans imagine themselves entering deep inside.

He brandishes the unpolished parts of himself as if they were a flag, a calculated weakness, going so far as to play with the fact of his own poor hygiene.[18] His little backwardnesses herald his arrival, function as his PR team, turn him into a logo: a little piglet. His vulnerability, a product. Here, a pink eyeshadow called 'Pig-ment'; there, a plastic mirror in the shape of a pig. At the heart of this story, we're all close – sisters, darlings, bitches, BFFs. The dividing line that separates us from influencers grows blurry in the face of the things we have in common, a muddy trench. We, too, are piglets; it's only natural that we'd buy pig-shaped merch, little effigies of Shane Dawson.

My uncle once told me that, when he was five years old, he cried for two weeks straight upon learning that human beings weren't made out of bologna but of flesh, of veins and organs, miniature mechanisms swollen with fluid that can and do stop beating without warning. That life, both big and small, is as fragile as glass.

18. From a Twitter conversation with Antoine Charbonneau-Demers, who wrote to me: 'I think it's calculated. I don't know [Shane Dawson] very well, but I know that he plays with the fact that he has bad hygiene. I think that's the reason for all the pig stuff.'

Beauty YouTubers, ostensibly vulnerable, offer a stark contrast to the predatory spirit of the big cosmetics manufacturers. Their ability to poke fun at themselves lends them an unpolished look – it gives their personas a less crafted, more genuine aura.[19] In order to create a sense of intimacy with the viewer, they put their weaknesses on display. When they cop to being hopeless at applying eyeliner, they're inviting us into that subterranean grotto, where love's secret pool shimmers. They want us to think of them as friends – not as fictional characters out to influence our spending patterns.

I've heard that astronauts, looking back at Earth from space, experience a sort of cognitive shock called the 'overview effect.' Because a trip into space allows for a singular view of our planet, it can lead to a kind of awakening, a widening of the astronaut's consciousness to take in an undeniable fact. Suddenly, the Earth looks vulnerable. It feels real in a brand-new way, like a naked heart, beating away in the infinite void. It's a pale blue dot, surrounded by a thin halo of atmosphere – a layer that astronaut Ron Garan describes as 'paper-thin.'[20] The overview effect forces the person experiencing it to recognize the precariousness of life on Earth. From space, it's possible to see the scars criss-crossing the planet's surface, places where erosion has taken hold, borders tracing its stencilled, yellowing flesh. Floating in a euphoric state, the overwhelmed astronauts feel themselves welling with love, with empathy, with care for the world. It makes sense – we love the things we perceive as vulnerable so that we'll take care of them. Is there anything as soothing as the knowledge that, somewhere, someone or something genuinely needs us? In this way, the spectacle of fragility is hypnotic. It's supposed

19. Giorgia Riboni, 'The YouTube Makeup Tutorial Video, a Preliminary Linguistic Analysis of the Language of "Makeup Gurus,"' *Lingue e Linguaggi*, No. 21 (August 2017): 189–205.

20. The Planetary Collective, *Overview*: https://vimeo.com/55073825.

to be the astronauts' favourite activity, this planet-watching – they love to stare down at us, drinking in the Earth's inherent vulnerability until they've practically got a buzz going.

Vulnerable things are especially susceptible to becoming the objects of memes, because they're easy to identify with – we recognize our own wounds in their bruised skin. We shout their vulnerability from our digital platforms because we see ourselves in them. It's a means of signalling who we are to others, of insisting they recognize us with a gesture, a word, a little bit of care. We, too, are searching for a kindness that will bandage our wounds. We, too, hope that someone, somewhere, will take care of us.

So I'm a cat affected by dwarfism, a falling girl, a haunting song. I show myself to others in morsels and band-aids. I hold in the palm of my hands my nicest shells, my bits of polished sea glass, green and blue. I share myself in odds and ends, in articles and songs, in poems and Facebook statuses. *This is my body – I give of it to you.* Ultimately, it's other people who turn me into a person, who gather the scattered pearls of me and string them into a necklace.

My vulnerability speaks directly to them, then – it asks for a little bit of tenderness, a little bit of attention, a little bit of care. The spectacle of the vulnerable – or, at least, its avowal – lends itself easily to the concept of sharing. It communicates a weakness, an echoing crack reverberating through other people's grottoes. We see someone else open up and find ourselves tempted to do just the same.

Vulnerability can also be a risky business, however, since to be fragile is to run the risk of suffering anew. All the better, because we must be able to welcome that eventuality, without which we're depriving ourselves of the possibility of being truly happy. We have to accept that we're always exposed to the knife edge of emotional pain, that it's likely to find our sore spots, to rummage around in our old hurts, widening the cut, deepening the crack.

'Mon amour, I'll never heal/if you keep fucking me in my wound' – a Josée Yvon line someone wrote on the wall in the women's washroom in a poet bar on Rue Saint-Denis.

But what does that consist of, exactly, fucking someone's wound?

The French word for healing, *guerir*, comes from the Germanic *warjanan*, to protect. I have no idea how to forge a shield for myself, though. All I can do is stack rocks and bread crumbs on my kitchen counter. I order some earrings from Japan and a new eyeliner. It's the colour of the moon, which is never far from my sight, that waxing and waning patron saint of lost souls – or, as you might call them, lunatics.

So here I am, with my satellite eyes, waiting for texts that won't come. Writing books in my head to tell my love who I am. To tell him who I am – yes, that's what I'm doing when I share a photo of some vulnerable little thing: a grumpy bear cub. A reject penguin. Just another animal, pining for love.

The French word for wound, *blessure*, meanwhile, derives ultimately from the Frankish *murthrian*, which means 'to assassinate.' *Mon amour*, I'm always in search of an assassin. Someone sharpied the shape of my gaping wound on the bathroom stall in a dive bar called Bistro de Paris. I thought I'd moved on, but here I am, a decade later, still picking at the same old scab.

I think about my sociologist. I think about the sugar daddies.

I wonder if anyone can tell that I wore that lingerie only once, that it just ended up on the floor, its lace already so bored with life. First come, first serve to hurt me, to make me blush, to change me. I'm so achingly vulnerable.

But it's the one thing I'm proud of.

We use vulnerability like it's a proof of good faith, the waxen seal of our individual truth. I am real because I'm capable of suffering – mortal, and breakable.

The imperfections inherent in Shane Dawson's persona, then, help us see him as sympathetic because of their amateurishness. He's relatable, common, pedestrian. Believable, human, 100 per cent real and authentic, full to the brim of this hollow authenticity we so badly wish meant something. Even to speak of authenticity can cause doubt to appear like a fissure in the nature of things,[21] can have us seeking out falsehoods in those around us like sharks sniffing for prey. Because, when we brand someone as inauthentic, we're signalling first and foremost the existence of its opposite – those who are fake or phony, '*fauné*,' as my friend Marie-Audrey would say.[22] But the real, the true, and the fake are all categories whose definitions are vague and ever-shifting. They're words dulled into meaninglessness by overuse, circulating and latching onto our legs and arms. We brandish them like Chanel handbags – the metonymy of a luxury that doesn't necessarily cost much to produce but that we recognize instantly, thanks to its logo.

In the Conspiracy webseries, Dawson describes himself as the victim of a string of injustices. He would never have known how to cash in on his influencer status, his 23 million YouTube subscribers. He's authentic, if not a bit naive – so pure that he couldn't even anticipate the carnivorous, bloodthirsty appetites of his business partners. Because he doesn't know how to play, he's getting played. He's incapable of recognizing his true symbolic worth, of comprehending just how much his fans love him. He says that he's often approached

21. After essays by Rob Horning, summed up in 'Mass Authentic,' *The New Inquiry*: https://thenewinquiry.com/blog/mass-authentic, published December 20, 2016.

22. TRANS. NOTE: Likely unintentional, but *fauné* is a homophone for *faux-né*, which means *false born* in French.

with unfair business deals – ones that he'd have happily signed on to, full of good faith. If Jeffree Star is to be believed, had Dawson learned how to properly value himself, he'd already have three houses by now, not one.

That calculus, of course, seems to suggest that true social injustice isn't a question of the sordid juxtaposition between abundance and lack, but one of an insufficient wealth, an affluence that might have been but never got the chance to truly spread its wings. It's in Conspiracy, then, we're led to believe, that Dawson first gets a chance to enter into an equitable business partnership. The real deal. This isn't just an eyeshadow palette – it's a cruel finger being taken off the scales, so that Dawson might receive his just reward. To buy a palette for yourself is to side with the masses of the real, the imperfect, the victimized.

Dawson's not a player – he's an open book. He's here, with concealer but without concealing, to speak his truth – out of the mouths of babes, or, at least, baby-faced influencers. He is transparency incarnate. As we see in the second episode of the webseries, 'The Secrets of the Beauty World,' he's not just here to sell makeup – he also wants to draw back the curtain and reveal the hidden underbelly of the industry. He's not one of the people involved in the cover-up – he's one of the ones exposing it, putting himself on display, a vigilante for truth.

When the last Conspiracy palettes sell out, the resellers don't hesitate. Their prices balloon, quickly hitting as high as three times the retail price. On Instagram, Star tries to dissuade his fans from buying from these scalpers. We must be patient and wait for it to come back in stock – to give our money to Shane, since he so clearly deserves it. Shane's worked so hard on this thing, Star pleads. To buy it is no longer a consumer act, it's an act of righteousness. We must repay he who has suffered. Better yet, it's a question of justice. Render unto Caesar his three houses!

While young buyers waste their hard-earned money at US$52 a pop, the disparities steepen and the desire for equality gets bogged down in the greenish greyish. The rich get richer, their houses stack up on top of each other, befurnish themselves, grow and gain pools, and are multiplied in triplicate. Coffee machines, pianos, and rugs appear; family photos pop up all along the mantelpiece. 'Excuse the mess,' the beauty influencers whisper, clad in dressing gowns, fresh from their king-sizeds.

And I'm staring at all the colours of Conspiracy. I'm staring at my own colours, the ones that make up my little aches, my handful of dried-up potted plants. My heart bleeds; it doesn't deserve a thing, not even a house to carry around on its back.

It's strange – almost counterproductive – to want to return order to the world by giving money to the rich. The poor get poorer; children keep on showing up for their shifts at the mines in India. Me, I'm the shrugging emoji. After all, living under the aegis of capitalism, I inhabit and engender the very same paradox.

¯_(ツ)_/¯

I read in a biology textbook that if you lock up a wasp with one of its larvae but no food, the wasp will chew off the larva's abdomen and feed it to the head so it has something to eat.[23]

23. C. Roux de Bézieux, *Les merveilles de la vie* (Paris: Éditions des Deux Coqs d'Or, 1962), 124.

Nobody understands the value of money better than those who calculate the prices of things in hours spent at work. The Conspiracy palette, at $52, costs a bit more than seven hours of minimum-wage work – it costs an early-morning awakening to the tune of *Marimba, or whatever that tone is.*[24] It costs a little fraction of something that can hardly be borne, since each awakening like this is a knife one plants in one's own back, a blow to a body that, over time, has become disillusioned with us, a lover we have ceased to love.

So we teach ourselves not to listen to these bodies of ours, because we have to ignore their cries in order to show up at work, punch in every day at the same time, and put our lives out to pasture for a barely tolerable salary. It's these bodies that Alex Noël spotlights in his article 'Les femmes invisibles' – the invisible women – which retraces the steps the workers used to take to the old Fruit of the Loom factory in Trois-Rivières.

'You had to watch them pour into *la shop*[25] in the wee hours. Six-hundred and fifty girls making their way to the Fruit of the Loom for the seven-thirty shift, 650 girls in the dawn hours of heat waves or the greyest November chills, 650 girls braving early-morning storms because the factory would never close so long as there were rollers of cotton to cut, so long as there were shirts and undies to sew up and to ship out.'[26]

24. Tara-Michelle Ziniuk, 'Retrograde,' from *Whatever, Iceberg* (Toronto: Mansfield Press, 2017), 70.

25. TRANS. NOTE: 'Shop' is an English word used in the original text, as it's common in Québécois French. Similarly, 'shift' in the original text is written as 'chiffre,' a francophone twist replacing the English word with a French soundalike, originally the word for 'number.' The adoption of English-language terms like this was a result of the socio-economic structure of Québécois factories in the twentieth century, where management was typically anglophone, while workers were typically francophone.

26. Alex Noël, 'Les femmes invisibles,' *Liberté*, issue 317 (2017): 62. Quote originally in French, my translation.

The Conspiracy palette costs more than money – it costs contempt. It costs silence and self-effacement. But when the chewed-off end of a larva puts on her makeup, she regains a little semblance of dignity. She regains possession of a little piece of that which cannot be borne, and her body – too often ignored, hen-pecked, filled to bursting, shoved aside – begins to glow. She knows how much a dollar's worth. That stuff she's putting on her eyelids is 7.17 hours of her life.

It's a far cry from the approximately ten seconds it takes Kylie Jenner – the world's youngest 'self-made' billionaire, lest we forget – to make $52.[27] A fleeting, transitory moment – a meteor streaking across the sky above L.A.

Approximately ten seconds is also how long it takes for Kylie to feel herself blush when the little thunderclap of shame she's carried since childhood strikes. The reality-TV starlet and Kardashian clan member isn't, after all, perfect – for a long time, she's been ashamed of her thin, curveless lips. One day, after what I imagine must have been a lengthy makeout session, a boy's impertinence confirms her suspicions. He said he was surprised that she was such a good kisser, considering how small her lips were.

That's all it took for Kylie to start finding herself ugly and undesirable. The lips – an erotic organ par excellence – allude to another set of lips, of course: the vulva. The latter, during sexual arousal, fill up with blood and darken – that is to say, they blush. Thus, lipstick is more than what it appears to be – it's a sort of visual double entendre, a racy reference to another opening, another mouth. It hints at what is to come.

27. According to this source, Kylie makes $19,006 an hour: Briana Trusty, 'How Much Money Kylie Jenner Really Makes in a Day,' https://www.nickiswift.com/169811/how-much-money-kylie-jenner-really-makes-in-a-day/, October 11, 2019. According to this one, she makes $19,007: Katie Warren, 'It Takes Kylie Jenner Just Over 2 Hours to Make as Much Money as the Average American Makes in a Year,' *Insider*, https://www.insider.com/kylie-jenner-earns-median-us-salary-in-just-over-2-hours-2018-8, August 8, 2018.

When he threw shade at her lips, did Kylie's crush deny her her full womanhood and plunge her back into her younger self? For cis women, the vulva carries a power – the power to transmit pleasure to its owner. Thus, the vulva is a form of independence – not an absence, not an envy of the penis, as a certain classic psychoanalytic theory holds – but an auto-erotic organ. The philosopher Luce Irigaray has even suggested that cis women 'are always "touching themselves" – they cannot, in fact, be prevented from doing so – because their genitals are made up of two lips forever kissing each other. She herself is already two [...] lovers.'[28] Not being able to kiss well, then, metonymically, would constitute a certain frigidity. Because she who cannot kiss others properly surely can't know how to kiss herself properly, how to love herself properly.

Shame pushes Kylie to an extreme recourse: injections, and from quite a young age. Again, the crack is widening. Like us, Kylie, too, suffers. She wants to be loved, starting with the love she should have for herself. It's humanizing, isn't it, to realize that no one ever feels like they're enough. After all, 'Who has not asked himself at some time or other: *am I a monster or is this what it means to be a person?*'[29]

In response to the shame, Kylie begins injecting herself and draws herself a set of full, curvy lips with a lip pencil. It doesn't take long for her newly swollen smile to fascinate her millions of Instagram followers. All around the world, her mouth becomes an object of envy – but also the butt of jokes. The term 'Kylie lips' shows up on Urban Dictionary

28. Luce Irigaray, 'Ce sexe qui n'en est pas un,' *Les Cahiers du GRIF*, Issue #5, 1974, p. 54. Translation is my own. Original quote: 'La femme "se touche" tout le temps, sans que l'on puisse d'ailleurs le lui interdire, car son sexe est fait de deux lèvres qui s'embrassent continûment. Ainsi, en elle, elle est déjà deux mais non divisibles en un(e)s qui se baisent.'

29. Clarice Lispector, *The Hour of the Star*, translated from the Portuguese by Benjamin Moser (New York: New Directions, 1992), 15.

to describe a curious phenomenon: 'when your lips are suddenly so big.'[30] The expression designates a particular kind of mutation – one that moves uncommonly swiftly, like a rabbit appearing from a hat that had seemed empty. That being said, this particular metamorphosis is a reversible one – after a few months, the effect fades, necessitating a brand-new injection.

In 2015, capitalizing off the buzz surrounding her newly iconic mouth, Kylie begins to market a combination of lip pencils and lipsticks that she calls Lip Kits. Because she claims that a sense of insecurity about her body led her to launch her brand, this might actually be the most authentic thing she's ever done.[31] One of the many faces of authenticity, then, must be the banal self-hatred we all direct at ourselves.

Kylie reifies the self-doubt that haunts her, crystallizes it into makeup, then into money. The resulting fortune seems good and true, then, almost wholesome, because it stems from a feeling of inadequacy, the kind that can seep right through the cracks of a person. It's hard not to respect the ambition of her gamble, to identify with the all-too-human feeling of never feeling comfortable, never feeling like you're enough. The savvy businesswoman knows that *there's a crack in everything – that's how the light gets in.*[32] But above all, she knows that it's possible to monetize that crack by generating a little bit of authenticity, that strange (and oh how lucrative!) alchemy.

30. https://www.urbandictionary.com/define.php?term=Kylie%20Lips, December 6, 2014

31. Zoe Weiner, 'Kylie Jenner Opens Up About Her Lip Injections and Starting Kylie Cosmetics,' *Teen Vogue*: https://www.teenvogue.com/story/kylie-jenner-lip-insecurity-kylie-cosmetics, May 2, 2018.

32. Leonard Cohen, 'Anthem.'

Makeup allows us to recreate the wound. It puts our frailty at centre stage, mimics the act of going to pieces. When we put on blush, when we apply lipstick, we're reclaiming our fragility, our capacity to let ourselves be changed by our surroundings. Our faces – under whose surfaces blood pumps ceaselessly – betray the ways other people make us feel, shout our insecurities across our skin. They're billboards for shame, for embarrassment, for arousal, for anger. Blood rushes to the surface of a pale carnation and evinces a momentary loss of control. We no longer have control over our bodies; they begin to speak without our consent. 'Death, power, and, of course, sex – the blush seeps into all,' Zoë Hu wrote in *The Believer*. 'As with weeping or fainting, it holds out the promise of a body that undermines itself, that can overwhelm a person into revealing certain physical truths.'[33] Isn't it dramatic to dissolve a little bit, to agree to change upon contact with another? For me, this drama is a force that shapes and undergirds the whole of my life. It's the very thing that permits me to go on loving. When I put on makeup, I'm highlighting my truth: I am vulnerable. And, as it goes in the Marina and the Diamonds song, 'Guess what? I am not a robot.'

We demand this vulnerability from our favourite influencers. We want our makeup gurus to be vulnerable, we want to see the cracks. We want chipped vases we can identify with. I don't just want Tati to show me how to make myself up or what to buy; I want to hear her false notes, to watch her cry, to hear about her endometriosis and her arguments, the mistakes of her wayward youth. I want her to spin the invisible thread that links the two of us together.

That way, if I buy her $48 palette, it's not because I'm out of eyeshadow, it's to proclaim my allegiance to her, this queen

33. Zoë Hu, 'Beauty Truly Blent,' *The Believer*, https://believermag.com/beauty-truly-blent, December 2, 2019.

of my wasted hours, to encourage the ostentatiousness of her vulnerability, the humanity she's putting on display. I'll support her to the end – through the darkness of her misfires, her sallow-faced vlogs, her hardships. I'm here. I'm buying. I'm here, because the spectacle of it all is so real.

A decade ago, the advent of Instagram fundamentally restructured how we see celebrity. Ordinary people, by becoming their own paparazzi, were able to attain a level of fame once reserved for the world's biggest stars. Among them were the influencers, those eminently visible people who began to profit off their cultural capital and ally themselves with brands in order to promote products on their various platforms.

An influencer's persuasiveness depends on the feeling of proximity and intimacy they're able to develop with their followers. It's an easy accessibility – they're forever just a tweet away, just a like away. In willing themselves closer to us, they've abolished the once seemingly impenetrable wall between stars and their fans. In French, the word for close, *proche*, is etymologically linked to the word for next, *prochain*. As if the next person to speak about lipstick in front of a camera might be me. When I watch these YouTube videos, in some sense I'm dreaming up a future for myself.

The era of the tabloids – where we once used to encounter un-made-up stars, crying, drunk, or unbalanced, shuffled off the stages of their own lives, where we used to laugh at the spectacle of their downfalls, where the goal was to capture their worst moments – is over. By contrast, the journalist Amanda Hess has suggested, Instagram is defined by an aesthetic of control. Influencers' lives take place in an entirely different reality, one where the image people have of each other is masterfully manipulated.[34] Even their most vulnerable moments are as staged as a movie shoot. Social media allows us to – and encourages us to – surveil and monitor the body and its extensions.

Whether we're sharing a picture of some washed-up driftwood or a perfectly made-up face, we are always the ones deciding how much of ourselves to show off to others.

34. Amanda Hess, 'When Instagram Killed the Tabloid Star,' *New York Times*, https://www.nytimes.com/2019/11/24/arts/celebrity-instagram.html, November 24, 2019.

Influencers exert a gravitational pull similar to the one reality TV stars have. They're just a multi-platform version of it, a Pokémon evolution. By responding to the dictates of authenticity, they permit us to develop a much more personal feeling of belonging toward the products we consume.

It's a mode of engagement that contrasts starkly with the general air of distrust that people hold toward faceless multinational corporations. Their slick, impersonal surfaces represent the polar opposite of the pore- and scar-covered skin I associate with my own. Authenticity, by contrast, rings of imperfection, of all that can be hurt or sickened, of that which bears the marks of aging, the imprints of life's hard knocks. In fact, we tend to think of authenticity in terms of the self – we judge others by how close or how far they seem from us, from the personal crosses we bear. Corporations, by contrast, seem essentially invulnerable. I tend to think of them as invincible, inhuman. They stand like colossuses, legs disappearing into the sky, antlers of smoke, grimaces of steel. I imagine them forming a perfect circle, cold and hard, chiselling out a moon-shaped hole in my grandmother Ghislaine's lungs. Arsenic, lead, sulphur dioxide. All I see is the distance separating us.

The language of business is riddled with conceptual metaphors that compare the economy to a hydraulic machine.[35] Economists write that it's 'starting up again,' or else overheating or idling, like an engine. Or you hear talk of liquidity, of diluting shares, of freezing funds, as if finance were water being pumped through the veins of the economy. All these words do is cleverly conceal the presence of the human body – that is, they erase the flesh-and-blood workers whose actions and decisions have a direct impact on the economy. As Pier-Pascale Boulanger writes: 'The truth is, there is no

35. Pier-Pascale Boulanger, 'L'argent est de l'eau. La machine de Phillips,' Observatoire du discours financier en traduction, http://odft.nt2.ca/blogue/l'argent-est-de-l'eau-la-machine-de-phillips, May 8, 2017. Translation is my own.

machine or motor – just agents who exist within power relations pursuing their material interests.'[36] The process of turning the financial sector into a non-human object benefits neo-liberal ideology in that it makes us believe in an economic system that could function without human involvement – almost a force of nature, like a river cascading over rocks. While this vocabulary has managed to detach economics from the human, it has also allowed large corporations to, in the collective imagination, become untethered from the human body, from its wounds and weaknesses. Now, without a tint of humanity, they've lost their powers of attraction, of persuasion. Corporations are no longer relatable – they're not your friend, not your grandmother, not even a pathetic little sloth waiting hesitantly at the side of the road. Rather, arrayed in convoluted forms, in shapeless and gigantic masses, today's companies tend to look more like LVMH Moët Hennessy Louis Vuitton, a firm with a portfolio that comprises over seventy different prestige brands. In order to graft a face back onto their metal hides, the colossuses, naturally, turned to influencers.

In the world of influencers, purchasing a product is seen as a special gesture, both unifying and intimate. You're not just buying a product, you're buying a flesh-and-blood person, the gift of their presence. And you'll keep buying as long as the emotional bond holds, because the love we have for other people is limitless, while the love we have for things can never be reciprocated. When you come to see someone as a friend, you don't just want to support them – you also want to enter into the communities they support, to integrate into their family. Makeup gurus never fail to remind us of that fact; they each have their own mantras to repeat, from Jeffree Star's 'Hi, how are ya?' to 'It's your girl, Jackie Aina!' to James Charles's

36. Ibid.

'Hi, sisters!' – the latter, of course, going so far as to trademark that sisterhood through his clothing line, Sisters Apparel. But taking advantage of the bonds of sorority to sell products is hardly a new strategy. By the end of the nineteenth century, cosmetics companies were pulling the very same trick, tapping into the semantic web of the family to approach their customers as sisters, or friends.[37] One such entrepreneur of the period, a Madame Yale, claimed she'd been entrusted with a sacred mission: she wasn't out to sell to customers, she was sharing with her 'sisters in misery'[38] a miracle product she herself had invented, a remedy for dull skin and sunken cheeks no doctor had been able to treat. In her brochures, Yale encouraged her customers to open up to her. Tell me all, everything,[39] she entreated them – your aches and pains, your little victories, your dark and lonely thoughts. This clever spin on mail-ordering took the form of an exchange of much more intimate letters over a century ago – but that very call-and-response behaviour is popular in today's influence industry as well. It's noticeable in particular in influencers' calls to action, those systematic solicitations of engagement that occur at the end of every video, when they slip in that familiar *Y'all will tell me what you think in the comments.*

At the turn of the twentieth century, beauty entrepreneurs – like Madam C. J. Walker, an African-American woman who was the first female self-made millionaire in the United States[40] – had to work on the fringes of retail, because gender- and

37. Kathy Peiss, *Hope in a Jar: The Making of America's Beauty Culture* (Philadelphia: University of Pennsylvania Press, 1998), 82.

38. Emmeline Clein, 'Madame Yale Made a Fortune with the 19th Century's Version of Goop,' *Smithsonian Magazine*: https://www.smithsonianmag.com/history/madame-yale-fortune-19th-century-goop-180974153, March 2020.

39. Kathy Peiss, *Hope*, 82.

40. 'First Self-Made Millionairess,' Guinness World Records, https://www.guinnessworldrecords.com/world-records/firstself-made-millionairess, consulted May 28, 2020.

race-based barriers made access to traditional distribution networks, or entry into supermarkets, typically stocked by white, male-run brands, near impossible.[41] Walker had to turn to going door-to-door – but it was in doing this that she first developed the relationship-based marketing techniques that would end up paving the way for a genuine cosmetics empire, one that saw her become not just a businesswoman but also a political activist and philanthropist, too. She made community the keystone of her financial success, spinning a web of flesh and conversation to hold close the women she sold her products to, and training thousands more door-to-door saleswomen like her, enabling many of them to achieve financial independence.

What many similar female entrepreneurs from the turn of the twentieth century teach us is that the then-fledgling cosmetics market was one of the first sectors to genuinely take advantage of sales techniques based on social ties, advice from 'friends,' mutual support, and care. I can't help but see, in the figure of someone like Walker, a kind of proto-influencer. Since they were able to give an emotional and social dimension to the sale of goods – to deliver not just products but advice and testimonials, too – these visitors were seen as peers rather than as saleswomen. Like Tati, Jackie Aina, or Makeup Kristi, who visit us in the comfort and privacy of our personal screens, the travelling saleswoman would meet her customers where they were: confined to their homes. She was a conduit between consumers and the faceless businesses, the metal colossuses. You could talk to her about your pimples, your sunken cheeks, or your hair problems, and in return, she made you feel – whether it was true or not – like she genuinely wanted to take care of you.

41. Kathy Peiss, *Hope*, 72.

Who took care of my grandmother Ghislaine? In love with a diamond driller who used to leave for work in Nepal for months at a time, she worked to raise three children on her own. In a letter home, he writes of an ox cart trip, of white rhinos, giant tigers, monkeys. He tells her that he's crossed a river without a bridge, that in the thick, leafy jungle *there are flowers as big as your washing machine*. Even though he ended every missive with kisses, one time he didn't end up making his way back. When my grandmother's heart broke, who took care of her? I wish I could go back in time, ring her doorbell, and steal her away from that dryer of hers – at least for an hour. I'd talk to her about makeup, or maybe poetry. I'd show her how to draw her eyebrows on.

Today, the work that influencers do is often belittled – or, as often as not, not recognized as work to begin with. There's a certain logic to that: the fruits of their labour are so often invisible. The primary product of an influencer is emotions, so the impact of influence – invisible and feminized as it so often is[42] – can be incredibly difficult to pin down. Unsurprisingly, the vagueness inherent to such a new sector of the economy as influencing makes for increasingly precarious work, with people often operating without the benefit of any real job security. Of course, many of them are hardly to be pitied: the standard image of the influencer raking in astronomical sums of money isn't a complete fiction. But not every influencer is Kylie Jenner. Because some are only micro-influencers or even nano-influencers (those with fewer than five thousand followers), it's easy to see how less privileged influencers might end up being taken advantage of, particularly in an industry where there is neither consensus nor transparency when it comes to earnings. But if the lifestyle that the top influencers luxuriate in is enviable and often lucrative, it's rendered more fragile by each successive scandal, a single one of which can mean the loss of tens of thousands of subscribers. The unstable nature of their work is also tied to the fact that it's necessarily embedded within the workings of private platforms like Instagram and Twitter. Influencers are forever at the mercy of external factors; their successes and failures depend on algorithms and technologies that can be changed in a blink. You might say that their careers are part of what sociologist Zygmunt

42. Affective labour (not to be confused with emotional labour, which is about managing one's own emotions) is work historically done overwhelmingly by women. It's a question of generating or effecting the emotional experiences of others. It's a type of labour that's growing increasingly important in economic terms, particularly when it comes to technology, where companies expend a lot of energy trying to grow their online audiences.

Bauman calls our 'liquid modernity' – a slippery reality that, as with any liquid, changes shape when the slightest external force is applied. It spills, flows, spurts all over the ground – just like the kind of relationships the sugar daddies want: no strings attached. They want babies who get wet for money, but no waterworks, please.

The emotional relationship between influencers and influencees is also one that's constantly threatening to break off. While any intimate relationship can sour in a heartbeat, these ones in particular revolve primarily around the sense of trust that influencers instill in their adoring publics. As a result, what people most often criticize influencers for is a lack of authenticity – the same sense of authenticity that once drew us right to them. When scandals do break, then, it's this quality in particular that must be singled out and scrutinized. It's common for influencers and their followers to go digging in their rivals' digital closets, searching for old racist tweets and other incriminating statements. These archaeological finds become weapons in a war of image, used to smear their enemies with shame and instill distrust. Faced with the incoherent jumble of shards of identity – fragments that don't remotely correspond to the perfect public image of the makeup guru they used to love – the disillusioned fans must now face the facts instead: the person in their screens was a stranger all along.

On June 12, 2019, Jaclyn Hill, a makeup guru in the online beauty community, posted an apology video that garnered more than 6 million views on YouTube. She was attempting to put an end to the heated controversy that had recently ensnared her So Rich lipstick line, the first product launched under the umbrella of her personal brand, Jaclyn Cosmetics. In the video, she speaks directly to the camera, seemingly un-made-up, her face naked in the ring light – as if appearing #nofilter were a symbolic pretense to her innocence.

This 'no-makeup makeup look' was of a piece with the unwritten rules that govern the 'apology video,' that genre in which an influencer addresses their audience and apologizes for crimes of being problematic, hoping to restore their reputation and maintain the loyalty of their subscribers. In such videos, the absence of makeup, naturally, evinces a more 'sincere' plea: one that is devoid of obvious artifice. The fewer filters there are, the easier it should be to feel close to the speaker.

Hill gives off girl-next-door vibes: the quintessential American girl, she grew up on a farm in Illinois before marrying her high-school sweetheart. A job at a MAC store led to her launching a YouTube channel, and then she blew up. After she'd amassed enough fans, a lipstick line followed. It wasn't a fairy tale story, though.

When the products launched, consumers started complaining about quality-control issues: black spots, a lumpy texture, hairy fibres and plastic particles embedded in the lipstick, and, horrifyingly, a concerning odour. The flaws were particularly surprising considering Hill had supposedly been working on the line for over half a decade. In the midst of a full-blown PR crisis, she tried to reassure her fans that nothing was wrong: 'My lipsticks are NOT mouldy. [...] They're not unsafe for you in any way, shape, or form.'

Hill's horror story made for fantastic viewing, and I, like many others, found myself wading into it. On YouTube, videos responding to the drama began to multiply, like cancerous cells in a tumour. I let the growth of them fill up my nights, these abnormal cells that came in twenty different shades of nude: Decaf, Hustle, Tipsy, Bada$$, and so on. I allowed myself to be carried away. I drifted.

'What exists at the bottom of this ocean? Shipwrecked vessels? Debris? The sea eats up everything. One day, any second now, it will eat me up too.'[43]

In response to the controversy, my favourite YouTubers started wearing lab coats and protective goggles; it seemed like the entire beauty community had begun to undertake a distinct shift into biochemistry. Those who were lucky enough to get their hands on the infamous $18 lipstick before it sold out got their investigator on. I watched them dissecting the little red tubes, armed with makeshift scalpels and microscopes.

All of this combined to propel 'science babes' like Kenna – a heretofore unknown cosmetic biochemist – to the fore. In a video shot in her parents' bathroom, Kenna walks her online audience through the laundry list of the lipstick's ingredients, discussing how it was manufactured and refuting several of Hill's apology-video assertions. Hill had claimed, for instance, that the hairs showing up in the lipstick must have been from the cottony gloves lab technicians had used to handle the tubes. But, according to Kenna, that kind of glove is never used in cosmetics labs – workers prefer nitrile or latex gloves.

The likes and views were stacking up. Everyone was interested in the dark side of the beauty industry: manufacturing. Suddenly, makeup aficionados began singing the praises of

43. Silvina Ocampo, *The Promise* (San Francisco: City Lights Books, 2019).

water- and fat-soluble ingredients. I was a sponge: I learned how to sterilize vats, how to recognize bacterial growth, the way rancid oil smells. Makeup was no longer just tutorials: all of a sudden, I was in chemistry class.

Onscreen, I watched these YouTubers blow off steam, taking their anger out on these shoddy tubes. There was something genuinely satisfying, even enjoyable, to all this unexpected destruction. Typically, wasting these oh-so-precious products is frowned upon. Here, now, I was witnessing an orgy – at least in the sense of Bataillean 'expenditure,' which is to say, the destruction of something excessive, an overrun. The glut of merchandise was destroyed, cut to ribbons, smashed and smeared. Goodbye to the makeup collection, goodbye to the very logic of accumulation. I watched as the beauty community burned up what Bataille calls 'the accursed share,' from whose ashes ecstasy rises. I was witnessing a sort of ritual sacrifice in the form of sanctioned rule-breaking, a sort of Purge. As we sliced and diced a little peach-pink tube, an idol slouched toward the stake.

JACLYN HILL IS A LIAR. WHY I BELIEVE JACLYN HILL IS A LIAR. JACLYN HILL IS LYING TO YOU. LIVE CHAT: WHY I'M CANCELLING JACLYN HILL COSMETICS.

The headlines all insisted on one thing: Hill had lied. She was no longer trustworthy. A month prior, another beauty YouTuber, James Charles, had lost millions of his own followers. The manicured hand of the market was making its intentions clear: the influencer is a highly volatile asset. And its value was plummeting.

If the bond of trust that unites influencers and consumers is forever on the brink of breaking, it's no wonder they're always in the throes of emotional upheaval. Convincing others of your good faith, putting your authenticity on display, is the apotheosis of affective labour. A few days after the lipstick controversy broke out, Hill added fuel to the fire of her disgrace: she disappeared completely from social media, deleting her Instagram and Twitter accounts. A victim of so-called 'cancel culture,' she opted to erase herself from the discourse – at least temporarily.

I read on Instagram that cancel culture – when a public figure is boycotted because of something they've said, done, or tweeted that's deemed reprehensible – internalizes and reproduces the logic of carcerality. It speaks of a desire to dispose of people, to remove them wholesale from society as we see fit. But, in fact, the logic and practices behind that desire are hardly new – they're carried out all the time on people we deem 'undesirable.' Muslim women in veils can't get jobs.[44] Black men are imprisoned at staggeringly high rates. Poor favelas too close to a planned Olympic park are razed to the ground. In the *Brown Daily Herald*, writer Quentin Thomas writes that, 'for those of us who seek to uphold social justice ideals, it behooves us to think about what it means for one of the mechanisms we access in the name of social justice – cancelling – to so closely resemble a system that produces negative life outcomes disproportionately for people of color.'[45] This means of monitoring and punishing situates violence at the level of the individual, rather than at the level of society. As such, it functions to perpetuate the trope of the 'isolated incident,' when the actions we're cancelling people for so often arise from social phenomena, inextricable from the systems they occur within.

44. TRANS. NOTE: In 2019, the Québec government passed a law, known as Bill 21, forbidding the wearing of religious garb by government employees. Couched in humanistic language, it was essentially a means of barring practising Muslims from jobs as wide-ranging as government functionary to schoolteacher. Protests ensued.

45. Quentin Thomas, 'Cancelling Cancel Culture,' *Brown Daily Herald*: https://www.browndailyherald.com/2018/11/06/thomas-21-cancelling-cancel-culture, November 6, 2018.

Too often, the drama that divides the beauty community feeds into cancel culture. These controversies undermine the influencers' promises of 'authenticity' and 'honesty' while simultaneously reinforcing the notion that it's possible for beauty culture influencers to speak the objective truth – genuinely, honestly, and selflessly. For that matter, the beauty community has its own 'drama channel': accounts such as Tea Spill, Tea by Ali, and Here for the Tea broadcast the community's most salacious gossip on a daily basis; they call it *spilling the tea*, a term appropriated from the Black drag community. In the videos these accounts publish, the suspects are accused of being liars, of being phony. Then there are the *receipts*, the incriminating screenshots that prove their guilt. Whatever the subject, whoever the accused, the crime at the centre of these controversies is always the inauthenticity of a public figure. We jab our fingers at them, accusing them of being corporate brands rather than real people.

But if authenticity is perennially in danger of being compromised, if it's forever under the microscope, it's because in accusing someone of inauthenticity, we're also reinforcing the idea that its inverse – the authentic – genuinely does exist,[46] that there really is a beautiful, true, and pure YouTube channel somewhere in the world. That there's such a thing as selfless, objective influencing.

46. Following the ideas developed by Rob Horning in the previously mentioned 'Mass Authentic,' *The New Inquiry*: https://thenewinquiry.com/blog/mass-authentic, December 20, 2016.

Under Jaclyn Hill's apology video, one YouTube comment stands out: 'Who's actually not listening to her but reading the comments while she babbles?' It's been liked over 51,000 times. In those likes, the truth emerges. We're less interested in what Hill has to say than in what her crisis has awakened: engagement.

As quickly as it was released, the So Rich lipstick line found itself subordinated to the even more fascinating by-product it spawned – that is, user-generated content. What kept me spellbound wasn't the makeup itself, it was the comments, the memes, the amateur dissection videos featuring women in makeshift smocks cutting up their makeup. My eyes drank in ultra-high-resolution shots of the lipstick, where I could discern, buried in its creamy flesh, all kinds of debris: black spheres, bits of metal, questionable fibres. I laughed at the horrified looks on the faces of YouTubers discovering that they, too, had bought contaminated product. It was the inevitability of these reactions that formed the marrow of the drama – this marrow that I sucked on, glued to my computer screen.

Today, the word *prosumer* (a portmanteau of *producer* and *consumer*) is used to describe the simultaneous acts of consumption and content production that are by now all too familiar to so many social media users. The figure of the prosumer is particularly apt when it comes to the beauty community, where each new launch represents an opportunity not just to consume but also to create content. In the wake of each product's appearance, tutorials devoted to teaching buyers how to use it will pop up, as will a host of video reviews all orbiting the eternal question: should we, or should we not, buy it for ourselves?

In fact, when I'm whiling away the hours in front of my screen, my favourite thing, above all, isn't buying things –

it's reading other people's product reviews. I can spend hours reading them: the one-star ones, the ones that say, 'If I could have given this zero stars, I would have.' I'm looking for negative-star reviews, veritable black-hole products. *The worst product ever! Breakouts! Fallout! Sheds! SLIPS OUT. Save your money, don't buy this.* I weigh the pros and cons of each potential purchase as the stars implode, feeling smug in my approach. I'm poring over the reviews of the users who've come before me, studying every detail of the products I covet. I imagine myself controlling these urges, keeping them on a leash, training them. Sit! Lie down! Shake a paw! I feel so free. As free as a dying star.

Kylie's first Lip Kits were gone in a flash, sold out within a minute of going on sale. Here, too, fans crashed the internet, overloading Shopify's servers and taking the app down. Parenthetically, it must be said that the initial inventory for releases like these is often kept intentionally low in order to generate an artificial sense of scarcity. When a quick sellout catalyzes the fans' FOMO, they stampede in a mad rush to buy as much of the product as possible. The less fortunate are left to pick up theirs from resellers charging exorbitant prices, and/or to run the risk of purchasing a counterfeit version instead. That's what happened to Khue Nong, a young woman who, in an interview for *Makeup Mayhem*, a documentary from Netflix's 2019 Broken series, claims to have bought what she believed to be a Lip Kit on eBay, only to end up with her mouth sealed shut with Super Glue.

The mass fervour for these ho-hum products – neither groundbreaking nor awe-inspiring – may seem surprising, especially when it ends with consumers like Nong putting their health at risk. But a Lip Kit is more than just a cosmetics cash grab – it functions as a link between Kylie and her fans. The ability to identify with her, the echoing 'me too' of our digital relationships, is actualized, then, via the acquisition of goods. It's an act of consumption that consummates the relationship between influencer and influencee – a declaration of love, sealed with a Lip Kit kiss.

On the back of her fans' greed, their love, and their FOMO, Kylie's empire has grown exponentially. After only a few years in business, she claimed to be the world's youngest self-made billionaire at twenty-one – edging out Facebook's Mark Zuckerberg, who hit the billion mark at age twenty-three –

in a 2019 *Forbes* cover story.[47] There she was, clad in a black suit, her arms crossed, a half-smile on her famous lips.

Kylie claims she quit using fillers in 2018, deciding she preferred a more natural look. It's as if, since the advent of Instagram, the selves we show to the world have become endlessly changeable, endlessly perfectible things. Full lips, like face filters, fade in and out of fashion. Our vision of beauty is as fluid as liquid eyeliner. We buy and reject different physical attributes in turn, our eyes attuned to the trends. In the words of journalist Amanda Hess, in our contemporary vision of femininity, the body can be 'endlessly upgraded for optimum sexual attractiveness,' functioning like software rather than hardware. In fact, there's a symbiotic relationship between beauty standards and the products on the market. Five or six years ago, we might have preferred full-coverage foundation; today, skin perfectors – super-light lotions that can barely hide a pimple – are all the rage. Physical features rotate in and out of style as if they were no more significant than social media accounts. Swollen lips: unfollowed. Angular eyebrows: blocked. Armpit hair: added as a friend.

One aspect of this consumerist, modular attitude toward beauty is a troubling relationship to race. There's a distinct racial ambiguity that courses through all of Kylie's empire – her shift to fuller lips and darker skin, traits that have historically been associated with Black bodies, is noteworthy.[48] Particularly given the fact that these same traits on people

47. A claim that the magazine has since walked back. See: Chase Peterson-Withorn and Madeline Berg, 'Inside Kylie Jenner's Web of Lies – and Why She's No Longer a Billionaire,' *Forbes*, https://www.forbes.com/sites/chasewithorn/2020/05/29/inside-kylie-jennerss-web-of-lies-and-why-shes-no-longer-a-billionaire, May 29, 2020.

48. In a 2018 *ID* article, Emma Dabiri wrote that 'today's most celebrated beauties are white women with augmented bodies and faces who've been cut and carved to produce a facsimile of blackness'; https://i-d.vice.com/en_uk/article/nepzyg/white-girls-instagram-blackface-blackfishing.

who aren't Kylie haven't led to billion-dollar fortunes but to stigma. Those women's lips aren't accessories; they don't represent an aesthetic choice, a product purchased. They are part of their bodies. Which raises the question: who, exactly, can afford to have a look that shifts and shimmers, a body that can be changed seemingly at will? This fluidity isn't just a class issue, it's also a race one. It's a question of who can take on certain characteristics without being stigmatized for them.

Of course, as the historian Kathy Peiss notes, 'cosmetics were never far removed from the fact of white supremacy.'[49] When I lived in Taipei, I had to scour my neighbourhood pharmacies just to find a cream that *didn't* brand itself as whitening. It was discombobulating to see my white privilege made tangible – here it was, arrayed all over the shelves. Where racism pushes people of colour to turn to cosmetics that seek to solve the problems of their bodies by minimizing them (to relax, to whiten, to constrain), it grants white people the inverse: the freedom to add on (to curl, to darken, to enlarge). As a white woman, I'm not asked to rein in my whiteness. On the contrary, I was taught to show myself off, to highlight myself, to write out my story in bold type.

In Taiwan, white supremacy wasn't just stocked in the pharmacies; it also paid my rent for a year. In 2012, I got a job teaching 'accent-free' English to four-year-old children in Taipei. Ironic, of course, since, as a francophone, my English is noticeably accented – but my white skin and blue eyes fit the bill. While a linguist might point out that there's no such thing as an 'unaccented' version of a language, no true neutral, in retrospect I think what my employers wanted wasn't my language so much as my ability to erase another one. I was being paid to teach children how to be something other than

49. Kathy Peiss, *Hope*, 203.

themselves, to make them believe in an ideal that could never be grasped, since, at its core, it didn't really exist.

So my students went through the motions, mechanically repeating the sounds I made. I was trying to teach them how to say *drawer*. 'Drawer, drawer, drawer,' we all said, struggling in unison. I understood how they must feel – even I began to hate my own French-speaking mouth for its inability to pronounce that weird, green-grey word. To my ears, it just sounded like murky water.

For her twenty-first birthday, Kylie Jenner released a cash-themed makeup line called the Money collection, replete with counterfeit $100 bills bearing her face – Kylie money. The products taunted me: one eyeshadow, a matte military khaki, was called Stacks, slang for a thousand dollars. Another was called Build Your Empire. It was performative workaholism,[50] the whole collection fuelled by the oh-so-American myth of meritocracy. Kylie's empire, by contrast, is built on a foundation of over 250 million Instagram followers, her eye-popping public profile a sort of inheritance from her participation, along with the other members of her family, in *Keeping Up with the Kardashians*. In financial terms, we might well consider her army of followers as simply one more in a collection of assets. In November 2019, when the Coty Group announced the purchase of 51 per cent of the shares in Kylie Cosmetics for $600 million, its CFO, Pierre-André Terisse, justified the transaction on the basis of her then-270 million followers, spread across a handful of platforms. 'With just one post, she can reach more than double the number of people who watch the Super Bowl every year,'[51] he said.

In a video entitled 'Official Kylie Jenner Office Tour,'[52] we watch Kylie stroll around her company's offices, practically out of breath as she makes her way from conference room to conference room. Entering empty rooms, she explains that

50. Erin Griffith, 'Why Are Young People Pretending to Love Work?', *New York Times*: https://www.nytimes.com/2019/01/26/business/against-hustle-culture-rise-and-grind-tgim.html, January 26, 2019.

51. Tonya Garcia, 'Coty's $600 Million Deal with Kylie Jenner Is Designed to Hang On to Her Social Media Star Power,' MarketWatch: https://www.marketwatch.com/story/cotys-600-million-deal-with-kylie-jenner-is-designed-to-hang-on-to-her-social-media-star-power-2019-11-18, November 23, 2019.

52. Kylie Jenner, Official Kylie Jenner Office Tour: https://www.youtube.com/watch?v=VayyLoioSAk&t=188s, October 10, 2019.

this is where the magic and the meetings take place. She talks about how necessary the cushy office chairs are, given her long working hours. Then, sitting at an oval table, she admits: 'The longest I've spent here is nine hours.' If it takes her ten seconds to make $52, nine hours is nearly $171,000. Kylie Money indeed.

By shooting in the workplace, emphasizing the materiality of her labour – the rooms, the tables, the office chairs – Kylie is talking to us about her work ethic, but she's also talking about her money. The money I have, she seems to be saying, came from hard work. By associating her wealth with this work, she steers the conversation away from her class privilege. It's an attempt to make herself seem more accessible. Isn't it nice to believe that a success like hers is within anyone's reach? One of her eyeshadows is even called Work For It. Conversely, for Kylie to own up to her privilege – that she launched her business with money and social status she did little, if anything, to earn – would be to pull back the curtain, to reveal the distance that really separates her from her fans. It's an insurmountable distance, a fault line, a crack that can open up and swallow you if you're not careful.

Is it any coincidence that the beauty market has absolutely exploded in an era when smart phones – and their cameras – are omnipresent?[53] Their ubiquity fuels 'selfie culture,' where the dominant social currency is pictures people have taken of their faces, but also more ephemeral snapshots, technologically manipulated pictures intended to mark the spot – *I was here* – and to enter into digital contact with others. Selfies aren't etched in stone, they're not attempts to immortalize moments of historical significance. They're fast fashion, intended for immediate consumption. In fact, you could argue, they're closer to a form of non-verbal communication, in sync with burgeoning digital conversational norms. The Québécois word for selfie, *égoportrait*, might suggest that selfies are portrait of our ego, but in reality, selfies are outward-facing. The 'self' in *selfie* is more reminiscent of reflexive pronouns (myself, herself, themselves, etc.). Taking a selfie necessitates not just action, but also one or more beings, establishing and maintaining a connection between far-apart people bound together by a common social interaction.[54]

Because the face, the sine qua non of the selfie, plays such an important role in our online interactions, cosmetics products aimed at it are experiencing a renaissance. Some, like Korean sheet masks, seem like they were created specifically to be shared on social media. They're like Instagram filters that have taken physical form; applied to the face, they allow us to slip into identities both silly and strange, and to mark an occasion: yes, we're taking care of ourselves – we're taking care of our skin. As Dalia Barghouty says in *Real Life* magazine,

53. Elaine Low, "How Instagram, Twitter Beauty Selfies Are Changing the Face of Retail,' *Investor's Business Daily*: https://www.investors.com/news/selfies-are-changing-the-face-of-retail, October 28, 2016.

54. Daphné B., 'le selfie,' *Spirale*: http://magazine-spirale.com/article-dune-publication/le-selfie, November 6, 2015.

'Makeup then works as not a tool of artifice but a way to manifest our being on and in relation to our camera lens, our screen, and ourselves.'[55] These days, I find myself increasingly making myself up with the promise of future selfies in mind. In fact, it feels like I'm always made-up, even in bed, my face oh-so-shareable, so camera-ready. And why not? My friends are much more likely to see my face smiling out from their feeds than they are to run into me in a café, because I spend my days working in my bedroom. But it's not just my made-up face that's onscreen in my photos; they're also a chronicle of the tapestry of my life being woven. By this point, my eyes have become adept at recognizing the 'documentary potential' of my day-to-day life, scanning through reality, looking for pretty things I can post. As Nathan Jurgenson puts it, 'The social photo initiates the process of documenting life so that you know how to see life when away from the screen.'[56] In essence, our eyes themselves become cellphone cameras.

And if I offer up my face to other people, maybe it's because it's simply the most legible part of my body. My eyes, mouth, nose, and forehead are fragments of a text written to be read by others. It's a text hidden from me, one I can only read through the prism of a reflection, when I see myself in the mirror.[57]

Women's faces are everywhere in our culture. The poet Susan Stewart argues, 'The face is what belongs to the other; it is unavailable to the woman herself.'[58] It's a text given meaning by those who look upon it, not by the person being looked at. We, the watchers, are the ones who give a face meaning,

55. Dalia Barghouty, 'Glow Aesthetic,' *Real Life Mag*: https://reallifemag.com/glow-aesthetics, August 22, 2019.

56. Nathan Jurgenson, *The Social Photo* (New York: Verso, 2019), 28.

57. Mary Ann Doane, *Femmes Fatales* (London: Routledge, 1991), 47.

58. Susan Stewart, 'The Imaginary Body,' *On Longing* (Durham: Duke University Press, 1993), 125.

and so the meaning fluctuates, just as the skin it is written in does. It grows red or gains wrinkles, tenses up or relaxes. Over time, it's transformed into *a map of marks and hair and age.*[59] It's not just a surface, it's a site of passage, a guestbook of the years. It keeps track of all that passes through it.

My eyes and mouth are crevices chiselled into the rock face – intimate hiding places that call out to every onlooker. I make myself up every morning, embellish these portals as if they allowed access to the underground pool of love, these caves filled with the unfathomable depths of the self. Do we read the text of a person's face or do we drown in it?

The face, it seems to me, is a much more intimate part of the body than the genitals. It speaks without speaking, in lip quivers and blackheads, in the openings of our mouths, eyes, nostrils. It's like a locket with a tiny photo tucked inside, or a dollhouse – there's something personal, something confidential, hidden in it. According to Stewart, dollhouses are the embodiment of a secret, a central core at the heart of a centre of its own: 'what we look for is the dollhouse within the dollhouse and its promise of an infinitely profound interiority.'[60] She also says that 'behind the appearance of eyes and mouth lies the interior stripped of appearances'[61] – as if, stripped of our skin, we'd be able to see who we really are. But 'beyond the perversion of the inside by the outside,'[62] as Derrida puts it, the mystery remains intact. Because if I scraped my own face off, all that would remain would be a mass of anonymous organs, a slimy brain that I myself wouldn't recognize, muscles, white and pink. There is no deeper meaning inside me, no true essence. What the openings in my face don't tell

59. Tara-Michelle Ziniuk, 'Divert,' *Whatever, Iceberg*, 78.

60. Susan Stewart, 'Imaginary Body,' 61.

61. Ibid., 127.

62. Jacques Derrida, *De la grammatologie* (Paris: Les Éditions de Minuit, 1967), 53.

you – or rather, what they do – is that everything is abyss. That meaning is not full but hollowed out. And that love is when an underground cave begins to fill with sea water, filtering in through a crack in the walls. Inside the grotto, all that can be heard is the sea and its echo. The sea and its echo. The sound of salty water brushing against the rock face.

We don't just stan these influencers because they're living embodiments of our dreams, chimeric hybrids of beauty and fame, but also because they represent expertise – they're authorities on the subject. They're called makeup gurus, after all, because of their know-how. They're like mahatmas; they don't just counsel us about purchases, they also give away spiritual advice. Their voices soothe me, their presence reassures me. When I witness the cracks – their anxiety attacks stacked between two cut creases and a little bit of blush – I want to tell them how much they mean to me. *You're a light in the darkness*, I'd tell them. *Even if you're only lighting my way – at least you're still shining*. They're really just lighting up my poverty threshold – the fine line between okay and not. Here I am in the doorway, taking delivery of yet another little box, covered in foundation, with my Sephora Red membership privileges and my free shipping, having spent over $1,000 on makeup this year.

Just like the gurus who populate my sleepless nights, makeup often does double duty. An eyeshadow palette is never just an eyeshadow palette; *ceci n'est pas un lipstick*. These products are so much more than just powders, creams, and lip glosses; makeup ads take care to remind us that these are all works of art. Which, honestly, I'm fine with. Isn't it much nicer to imagine you're buying a pretty painting than a greenish-greyish wad of cash and guns? Who wants to be responsible for the koalas dying off or a war breaking out? I want to celebrate my creativity, to support the arts. They're one of the few things with the power to make human beings seem a little less loathsome.

It's in the cosmetics industry's best interest to make this form of expression an unshakable, almost transcendent, value. Call something 'art' and it's suddenly beyond reproach. That's why Shane Dawson and Jeffree Star devoted a significant chunk of their web series to designing their palette like painters hovering over an easel, taking care to film themselves in the process of deliberating over colour choices, deep in what seems like a creative trance. That's why they spend so much time designing the packaging, mining moments of genius from their mountains of sketches. They want us to believe that the thing slowly taking shape before our eyes isn't just another knick-knack spat out by the conveyor belt of capitalism, but a kind of sacred idol, a thing to be worshipped. Months later, in the midst of a global pandemic killing Americans by the hundreds of thousands, Star will be dragged online for launching the Cremated palette, with its cool, ashy hues, and eyeshadow names like 'R.I.P.,' 'Casket Ready,' and 'The Morgue.' Star's defence is to play the *artiste*: his palette is much more than a product, it's an opus. We can interpret it however we want, he seems to say, but its core message is positive. Star wants us to grant his commercial production the right to be read as an artistic process, a personal journey with benefits for one and all. He's painting with the same brush Kylie Jenner used to disguise the ugly secret of her untold wealth. In the guided tour of Kylie Cosmetics, of course, she makes sure to stop in front of her 'iconic Lip Kit wall,' a floor-to-ceiling shimmery gradient of different Lip Kit packages. 'This is another way to use my products and make art with them,'[63] she says. A sort of trompe l'oeil.

When the commercial object doubles as an art object, the container is as important as the substance inside. We see this in the work of Swiss artist Sylvie Fleury, who covers her canvases with giant makeup palettes; *Road Movie*, one of the paintings in her 2018 *Palettes of Shadows* series, for instance, is a Chanel eyeshadow box, with its colourful dots and cube shape. So faithful is the recreation that you're

63. Kylie Jenner.

almost tempted to dip a brush into it – though, of course, it's only an image.

Is it art? Or just cosmetics? The seductive power of a plastic-packaged splendour? Is this freedom? Because my road movie isn't a Chanel palette. It's a hunk, his hair blowing in the wind, day-tripping down the highways of America. Tracing a route bathed in sunsets and dust. His ride won't stop for anything, not even death, because my road movie always ends by driving off a cliff. It presses the accelerator. It presses any key to enter. SEND, ENTER, START, YES, ACCEPT, BUY, BUY NOW. I watch my road movie fall to his death. I stare into the void. It's gold, burnt sienna, sky blue, and opalescent, and always hungry for more.

Remember when the anarchist pop star had a baby with the billionaire's son?

There's more to the love story than that, says Anne Boyer. There's also a beast – and it's not the baby. It's something that lurks everywhere, from the frame of Fleury's *Road Movie* to the depths of my laundry basket. It's present in every bedroom in the world, in every river in America, in every dirty apartment, in every half-empty refrigerator. It's in between the cushions of unfolding sofa beds; it's in the cigarette burns on smoke-scented couches, the air that fills inflatable mattresses. It's hiding in mould-black bathrooms, in holes punched through walls, and stuffed in the pockets of children sent out to buy milk at the corner store, next to their pocket knives. The beast growls, and you know it means it. 'There's a brute in these rooms and apartments and duplexes and trailers and shared houses and single-family houses and estates. The brute is not human, but like a bear, if a bear were a shadow and ten times bigger than a bear. This brute like a shadow and a bear not a human is named survival-life.'[64]

It's in the shadow of this creature that so many people make themselves up. It's in all my products – my shiny little potions, my secret samples, my heavenly powders. It watches me when I put on my face every morning. Because makeup isn't just the greenish-greyish wad of cash and guns. It's a bit of dignity, of humanity, even. It's also what gets me through the day. It's one facet of the beast that is life in survival mode – a form of enforced existence. Because at night, as Boyer says, we fall asleep in the bear's arms.

Remember Schmoney? The dirty green eyeshadow, unchecked capitalism in powder form? It's the bastard child of another term: *shmoney*. Shmoney is the underground, it's the resistance. It's the genuine article, real punk rock. The

64. Anne Boyer, 19.

makeup's name is a cheap adaptation of an African American slang term. Just scratch off the C to reveal its true heritage, its function as a weapon of survival.

I learned the truth on UrbanDictionary: *shmoney* means dirty money, crooked money, under-the-table money. It's right there in the name: money that says 'shhhh,' asks us not to tell. 'Shh! Quiet. Don't make a sound.' Otherwise, we're done for. Shmoney is the everyday risks people face trying to keep their heads above water. People doing the best they can with what they have. People who hustle. 'Hustlin's doin whatever you gotta do to get that paper,' says an UrbanDictionary comment from a user named Painn in 2008. It's got over six hundred likes.

#shmoneydance #hustling #shmurda #gucci

In July 2014, the rapper Bobby Shmurda released the music video for 'Hot N*gga,' his debut single. It features the then-twenty-year-old rapper smoking, drinking, throwing up gang signs, surrounded by his crew. In short, standard rap video fare. What set it apart from other videos was a dance: twice in the video, Shmurda and his sidekicks bust a series of moves that will become so popular, they'll propel the track to sixth place on the Hot 100 list. A rising star is born. The dance is called the Shmoney Dance, a hip- and elbow-focused celebration of their ill-gotten gains. His shmoney's burning a hole in his pocket – he spends it as quickly as he makes it, striking back against the survival-life that he's lived, that mode that looms large over the poor with its enormous ursine shadow. He wastes his shmoney, renders unto evil what is evil's, loads it into the guns he's bought with it. He sings of his dead friends, his imprisoned father, the crack he's been selling since the fifth grade. It's Bataille again: the orgy of excess money being burned off, the righting of an unspoken wrong. It's a middle finger to the system, the crooked scales that have governed his existence since he was born, a big *fuck you* to his own accursed share.

Shmurda's vengeful glee is contagious. In short order, his dance moves are everywhere online, looping over and over, especially on the now-defunct video-sharing app Vine. The Shmoney Dance is catching. It spreads like wildfire. It's getting remixed, replayed, reinterpreted. Even Beyoncé wants a piece, using the song in concert.

What's particularly striking about the 'Hot N*gga' music video is just how young Shmurda is. His goofy teenage grin, his frail teenage frame. He looks like someone's younger brother, swimming in his too-large pants, singing of his too-large guns. He raps about his hustle almost candidly, interspersing his life story with flashes of shmoney. Just because it's supposed to be quiet doesn't mean you can't dance to it. But he's still a child.

Which doesn't stop him from being arrested just a few short months into his new-found stardom. The police are out to put a stop to his victory dance. There's an official story, but Shmurda disputes it. In an interview, he opens up about the real reason for his arrest: 'The day they locked me up, they said, "We're tired of our kids listening to your music." They said it to my face, laughing.'[65] The arrest was the end of Shmurda's meteoric rise. Thereafter, his career seemed to drift off, like a person falling into restful slumber, warm and cradled by a giant bear – that bear who's not really a bear, a bear called *survival-life*.

65. Robert Kolker, 'Hot Shmurda,' *Vulture*: https://www.vulture.com/2015/05/bobby-shmurda-court-case.html, May 4, 2015.

Yes, makeup is too often greenish greyish, too often schmoney – the repulsive complexion of wealth.

But its colour is always in flux and never limited to a single shade. Makeup is complex, almost phosphorescent; it glows like a lantern, or a firefly in the night.[66] It's a symbol of resistance, a flickering light striving against all odds in the darkness of the great bear's shadow.

The flickering light of survivors is a faintly illuminating beacon. In fact, Georges Didi-Huberman writes that the image of the firefly is 'characterized by its intermittence, its fragility, its pulse of appearance and disappearance, of reappearances and redisappearances without end.'[67] Sometimes cosmetics, like the fireflies dotting the night sky, 'teach us that destruction [...] is never absolute,'[68] that capitalism can never steal the entirety of our lives, of our bodies. The time I devote to making myself up, for example, is a sort of time suspended in time where I turn inward toward myself. I'm so used to dissecting my days, slicing up the minutes and hours, trying to squeeze ever more money out of them – because I've learned the trick, as Foucault says, 'for turning to ever-increased profit or use the movement of passing time.'[69]

Some days, it feels like my life – my time – is a material object, a Rubik's Cube–like enigma I'm trying to solve with my hands, forever trying to get the colours to all line up. Like all I am is a human to-do list, crossing myself off, one task at a time. My twin sister is a ceramicist. Like me, she's forever on a money treadmill, trying to catch up to a living just out

66. Here, I'm borrowing the concept of the 'survival of the fireflies,' explored by Georges Didi-Huberman in his book of the same name.

67. Georges Didi-Huberman, *Survival of the Fireflies*, translated from the French by Lia Swope-Mitchell (Minneapolis: University of Minnesota Press, 2018 [2009]), 43.

68. Ibid.

69. Michel Foucault, *Discipline and Punish*, translated from the French by Alan Sheridan (New York: Pantheon Books, 1977), 157.

of reach. While she's off selling her wares around Montreal, I'm at home doing my best to finish up all my freelance translation gigs. Do rats in a maze eat for pleasure, or just out of a sense of obligation? When my sister and I get overwhelmed, we turn to Ensure – you know, the protein drink for people on their deathbeds. Keeping myself alive is just one more item on a to-do list. And I only started using to-do lists because they're supposed to help with the jaw-clenching.

My days are a series of boxes to tick off, dates to remember, appointments to make, deadlines to meet. When I was studying literature in university, no one ever told me that I'd need to learn how to juggle just to free up some time in my schedule for writing. Like so many writers, I do succumb to the cult of productivity at times. But when I call it out, it's because I know what it does to people, the ravages it puts my citalopram-riddled body through. The art world is full of ambitious and overproductive try-hards and people who think a forest-sized collection of potted plants might just keep them from growing bitter with age. Unless you're lucky enough to win the lottery or to be born a billion-heir, creating under late capitalism is a permanent hustle, an endless quest for resources. We cannot escape the society we were born into. It's like living close to the Chernobyl reactor in the aftermath of the nuclear disaster. Cesium radiation may be invisible, but it passes through humans all the same, subtly altering their molecular structure. As one townsperson put it, 'We wanted to hide from the atom as if we were hiding from shrapnel. But the atom is everywhere. In the bread, in the salt. We breathe radiation, we eat it. [...] Then how can we live?'[70]

70. Nikolaï Prokhorovitch Jarkov, quoted by Svetlana Alexievich, *Voices from Chernobyl: The Oral History of a Nuclear Disaster*, translated from the Russian into English by Keith Gessen (Illinois: Dalkey Archive Press, 2005 [1997]), 124.

For me, the escape from the monetization of time is in makeup. Mirrors don't have second hands, minute hands, hour hands. In front of my mirror, I stop trying to be productive with my time, stop trying to cash in on it. Sometimes I get all dolled up without even getting out of bed. I spend the day in my room doing freelance work, under the covers and out of sight. In fact, when I put on my powders and creams, I find myself feeling a little closer to my body after ignoring it my whole life. I'm returning to it a sense of importance, of dignity. I smile at it, put some blush on its cheeks. I take care of it – of me, of us. I split myself in two. Makes it easier to hug myself.

For a few seconds, I stop trying to apologize to anyone else, despite the ever-present 'sorry' hiding at the back of my throat. Sorry for what? For being alive? Every morning, I turn my waking hours into a kingdom of brushes, cotton swabs, and tiny jars that smell so sweet – a sacred space where I feel like a fledgling bluebird, forever learning to fly. I file off, comb through, and polish over all that is human and fragile within me. I love my body, this thirty-year-old woman's body, this body that was hit and strangled as a child. I tear those violences down from the walls of my memory and put up colours instead. To the words that still echo in my head – the *sluts*, the *bitches*, the *little whores* lodged deep in my psyche – I say: no. I'm taking myself back, back from the words that wanted me dead. Look at this body, now, finally standing up straight, how beautiful it is. So let it waste a little bit of time, if it wants to, trying to look like a bird. Because in giving myself back that time, I'm also giving myself life.

I want to be lusted after and I want to be loved. So often, though, my makeup has felt controversial. Like my poems, which a literary critic once deemed no better than 'glinting surfaces,' it's even been laughed at. All that glitters is dazzling, might blind you if you stare at it too long. Shiny, glossy surfaces, like made-up faces, take heat for concealing the truth, for making it that much harder to get at. From this perspective, makeup isn't just creams and powders; in Jacqueline Lichtenstein's words, it reveals 'the truth of the body as appearance.'[71] Like the way figures of speech and vividly imagistic words force us to recognize the truth of the poem as writing.

In any case, whether they're literary critics or would-be lovers, the men in my life all seem to want to point out my transgressions. To them, I've always been the girl who overdid things, who went too far, my face full to overflowing with desire. I guess they would have preferred plain, low-fat yogurt to my full-flavour, fruit-on-the-bottom approach. It's not in good taste to be tasty.

Why do you put on so much makeup? It's ugly. You shouldn't wear so much.

Was my full face more like clown makeup? A text of purple prose that I'd gone to all that trouble to highlight, as if I was trying to make some kind of point? What was it these men had read on the billboard of my face? Did they see the slogans bragging about the tenderness I showed toward myself with my self-care routine, hunched in front of the mirror every morning? I guess it didn't matter. When they criticized my makeup, it felt like they were spitting on the poem of me. They were awarding me stars only to take them back, wiping their feet on my doormat skin.

71. Jacqueline Lichtenstein, *The Eloquence of Color: Rhetoric and Painting in the French Classical Age*, translated from the French by Emily McVarish (Berkeley: University of California Press, 1993), 39.

Isn't it ironic how lazy girls somehow always manage to overdo things? Wandering the wilderness, dragging both the 'chick lit' novels and the book-length text messages we write behind us. We're not worth much, lackadaisical girls like us – certainly not so much as three stars. Overly repetitive, caked-up, be-powdered, and artificially lengthened, with our extensions clipped onto the backs of our heads.

These days, though, I know how to shut those critics down. I'm getting quite practised at it. I understand, now, that my body belongs to me alone – that I'm writing out the poem of it for myself, first and foremost.

Since at least the time of Plato – who condemned *kosmêtikê* as a search for borrowed beauty – makeup has been seen as a harmful thing, because it's inherently deceptive. As Jacqueline Lichtenstein writes, 'An entire tradition, of which we are the heirs, takes cosmetics to mark an original defect, to veil an ugliness always sensed beneath the virtuosity of masks, to signal an imperfection that art seeks to dissimulate.'[72] If I were to take Plato at his word, I'd not only have to consider myself a liar, but also the bearer of a curse, an original sin, a stigma I try to erase from my face each morning.

That tradition Lichtenstein speaks of has real-life consequences. We tend to mock made-up faces that call attention to themselves, rather than praising the artistry they so clearly demonstrate. We like to make fun of girls who 'cake it on' because their looks are artificial – diametrically opposed, then, to so-called 'real' beauty. Like poetic language, makeup is elegant up to a point, past which it becomes overdone, in bad taste. Maybe that's why, one day, an author I was talking to about my interest in makeup was so quick to tell me that she'd never worn makeup in her life, and how proud she was of that fact. What did that make me, I wondered. A childish nuisance, a master illusionist, a two-bit magician with winged eyes but no doves?

The truth is, makeup is most acceptable when it's in hiding, when it succeeds at obscuring all the work that went into it. We tolerate artifice best when it's doubly false – when it camouflages not just the face but its very presence as well, when it looks natural rather than flashy. We all love a 'no-makeup makeup look,' one that subtly sublimates a person's pre-existing beauty without drastically modifying their features, that wears an invisibility cloak and covers its own tracks. We don't want metamorphosis, but rather a delicate

72. Jacqueline Lichtenstein, *Eloquence of Color*, 42.

glow-up, a light touch of makeup that could pass for real skin, a near-invisible layer trying its best not to cry *Liar!* in a crowded room. Lichtenstein again: 'Ornament must not be seen but must make its object visible, it must show without showing itself.'[73] In essence, it must show without showing off. This, they say, is good taste.

More than two thousand years ago, the Roman poet Ovid, a budding mansplainer, advised women to put on makeup as discreetly as possible: 'Don't let your lover surprise you, with all your little boxes lined up on the table! Use them in secret,'[74] he says in a section of his *Amores* called '*Medicamina Faciei Femineae.*' Makeup, which he sees as a necessary evil in the war of the sexes, is still, for so many men, a shocking reality. So he asks all the female soldiers to pretend the war is just a fiction, that there's no conquest to be made. Only men have the right to wage war like this, constantly seeking out new territories to conquer – because if women are seen as deliberately trying to please, they run the risk of being confused for a *meretrix*, a sex worker. The obscenity of cosmetics is twofold, then – not just because it highlights a feminine pleasure-seeking, but also because it allows women to have control over their own images, to be the tellers of their own stories. All those little boxes lined up on the table represent a wealth of knowledge – sophisticated techniques and skills – that can seem threatening to the uninitiated, the way a magician's tricks can truly seem like magic.

Once, a few years ago, a man I'd been talking to came over to my place, purportedly to do some tech support for me – my computer was acting weird. When he came back from the bathroom, his whole face had changed – a mix of surprise and disgust. He mentioned the three Mason jars full

73. Ibid., 185.

74. Ovid, *L'Art d'aimer*, translation and adaptation by Michel Grodent (Brussels: Éditions Complexe, 2005), 86. Translation my own.

of makeup brushes lined up above my sink. He never called me again.

As beauty writer Arabelle Sicardi says, 'Men want beauty, but they don't want to see the work; they don't want to see the space beauty takes up.'[75] We love the idea of a beauty that naturally conforms to pre-existing aesthetic standards without requiring any outside intervention, any technological support – a beauty that's natural and effortless. We want virginal blondes, but we don't want to hear a word about peroxide. We want skin that doesn't need any cream to stay soft, we want legs that don't need a razor to stay smooth. We want so badly to believe in an impossible perfection, even if it means being lied to, as long as we never find out. In fact, the problem is conceptual – there's an inability to conceive of beauty as a constructed thing, even if people recognize that it's something that shifts and changes according to time and place, even if it has always required work that takes up very real time and space. It also makes noise – a quiet, metallic clicking, for example. The cosmetics manufacturer Guerlain is famously said to have tested dozens of different lipstick-tube models before settling on one quiet enough that public touch-ups wouldn't attract undue attention. It's a bit of corporate fastidiousness that isn't impressive or funny to Sicardi so much as it's a way of invalidating women's experiences yet again, yet more proof that 'the reality of women's existence in the world has been shaped to be seen, never heard; witnessed, but never believed; desired but never trusted.'[76] I get it. Sometimes I wish I could scream how much it costs to be cute, how many hours I've spent waxing my

75. Arabelle Sicardi, 'Beauty Is Broken,' *Medium*: https://medium.com/matter/beauty-is-broken-62dfd2be69df, December 10, 2015.

76. Arabelle Sicardi, 'A History of Lipsticks as Warfare,' *The Cut*: https://www.thecut.com/2018/10/a-history-of-lipstick-as-warfare.html, October 12, 2018.

bikini line, removing hair from my upper lip, conditioning my locks, blushing my cheeks. To tell all those who like my selfies – who comment 'gorgeous,' or strings of emoji hearts, to those who look in the mirror only when they're brushing their teeth – how much collecting all their comments costs me. I want them to know that fantasies this convincing are expensive. I wish I could show them the Mason jars full of brushes above my sink. That, too, would be a selfie. And who really benefits from my hiding them?

While the labour takes up time and space, its products are mostly invisible: emotions. Intangible goods that, nonetheless, are quite powerful, capable of influencing the flow of capital and disrupting the fabric of society itself. During the Second World War, British, American, and Canadian women were encouraged to look good to boost the morale of the troops. This dovetailed with the production of lipsticks – Victory Red, Regimental Red, and Commando[77] – that represented a war effort with collective and concrete psychological fallout. At the time, wearing red lipstick became more than a fashion statement: it was a symbol of strength and patriotic pride. So then yes – militarized and instrumentalized by the state, makeup *can* be recognized for the labour that it is. I've never been pressed into service by an Uncle Sam poster, but I've been a waitress before, and it doesn't take an image consultant to understand that your appearance plays a big role. By following certain aesthetic codes and performing the labour of beauty, from the hiring process to the restaurant floor, you show everyone that you're aiming to please. Servers stage a form of care like a play: we put on a concern for others, a sort of respect for the gaze that falls

77. Marlen Komar, 'Makeup & War Are More Intricately Connected Than You Realized,' *Bustle*: https://www.bustle.com/p/makeup-war-are-more-intricately-connected-than-you-realized-51078, October 28, 2017.

upon us. So I would smile at my customers, feign a good mood, and pretend to laugh at their terrible jokes. Servers aren't just the backs, arms, hands carrying out your orders – they're also eyes, mouths, ears ensuring your good time. *This is my body, I give of it to you.*

I have a date with a sugar daddy tonight. Putting on my makeup reminds me of the choreography of self-care I used to practise on myself before a shift at the bar, of the steps to that dance I used to do where I gave myself away for next to nothing. The trick is to listen to music: Tupac, disco, anything that pumps me up. I imagine that I'm on my way to a party where someone has promised me I'll have the time of my life, hot stuff.

My room becomes a dance floor – at least, until I catch my chubby legs and cankles in the mirror. I'm a far cry from a model. I wonder if I should give this sugar daddy a discount. Or maybe my two master's degrees mean I'm a rare commodity – a babe with real brains. Knock on wood, I tell myself, and reach for my plywood dresser. I glance again at the mirror, searching for flaws. Some anarchic hairs jump out at me, though it's been a quarter of an hour now that I've been waxing them away. I'm wasting my time. There will always be imperfections, visible pores, traces of my fiction, the acrid smell of my anxiety. Maybe I should give him a discount. I play 'Disco Inferno,' 'Ring My Bell,' 'I Love to Love' to distract myself, but the question keeps coming back to haunt me: should I give him a discount?

The social and economic importance of physical desirability goes well beyond the scope of sexual attraction, but it hasn't always played so central a role in our lives. It wasn't until the beginning of the twentieth century that it gained an importance that more closely resembles the one it holds today. The turn of the century was a period when the criteria for evaluating one's romantic partners went through noticeable changes, becoming much more diverse. Endogamy – the term for marriage that occurs within one's own social group – was becoming much less popular. In-group status was no longer a strong predictor of marriageability; more than ever, people wanted a spouse with sex appeal, someone whose beautiful smile – whose glinting teeth, whose flashing biceps – you'd swipe right on on Tinder. Since then, physical beauty has only gained in importance – and with it, anything that will grant us access to it. It's no surprise that we find the twenty-first-century cosmetics market absolutely flooded with products.

Today, physical beauty continues to hold the promise of love and social mobility. Its ability to forge new alliances can transcend social class – to marry a prince, you no longer need to be a princess. You just have to be beautiful. As author Eva Illouz puts it, 'Thanks to the demise of formal mechanisms of endogamy, through the transformation and individualization of sexual practices, and through the intense valorization of sex and beauty via the media, the twentieth century witnessed the formation of a new capital circulated in sexual fields that we may call "erotic capital."'[78] When you apply makeup, your value increases; the coefficient of your desirability goes up. Eroticizing the body is a time-consuming process, one whose progress can be measured in hours spent at the gym toning your abs, or in front of the mirror

78. Eva Illouz, *Why Love Hurts* (New York: John Wiley & Sons, 2013), 55–56.

straightening your hair. It's not all expense, however – it's an investment, one that can pay off big, because the more attractive you are, the more preferential treatment you receive – privileges, generous tips, free passes both figurative and literal.

Unsurprisingly, the burgeoning importance of erotic capital paved the way for advertising campaigns that explicitly linked cosmetics to sex appeal. Consider Revlon's 'Fire and Ice' campaign, one of the first of its kind. Launched in 1952, its ads for a matching lipstick and nail polish were a historic success. The campaign was targeted at so-called 'women of fire and ice.' Who is this woman? She's a legendary creature, forever caught between the twin poles that circumscribe female glamour: Virgin and Whore. I know her well. She's the woman I've always wanted to be.

One ad in the campaign paired a full-page photo of a star in a sequined dress with a little proto-Buzzfeed quiz: fifteen questions to help determine whether you, too, qualify as a woman of Fire and Ice. Tick off eight or more yeses and you're in:

> *Have you ever danced with your shoes off?*
> *Did you ever wish on a new moon?*
> *Have you ever wanted to wear an ankle bracelet?*
> *Do you secretly hope the next man you meet will be a psychiatrist?*

Me, I just got back from therapy, with all the glamour of a woman still in her PJs, eating a sandwich, scrolling down the rivers of Instagram for an hour. Still, I want to let Revlon know that I, too, like to play with fire, and I, too, like to skate on thin ice. Yes, Revlon, gypsy music does make me sad, and yes, Revlon, if I could fly to Mars then I would, and go full tourist. Yes, Revlon, I am the kind of woman who says, 'To hell with the recipe,' and adds two dashes of bitters instead of just one, yes, I do dance barefoot, and yes, I do close my eyes when I go in for a kiss. Yes, Revlon, fur does turn me on, particularly on other women's bodies. I, too, blush when I flirt, and at crowded parties, I, too, panic at first and then invariably end up having a great time. Yes, yes, yes to every question, I absolutely would go platinum blonde on a whim, without ever consulting my husband. It is I, Fire and Ice woman. I raise my hand, as if asking for permission to speak, and whisper a quiet 'Yes' into the emptiness of my apartment.

Fifteen yeses later, it feels like Revlon's become a part of me, has travelled deep within me, gone to speak to my inner child's truest wishes. She's singing, her wrists encircled with friendship bracelets; she dreams of bare feet, platinum blonde locks, and crowded parties. She doesn't know yet that at the heart of the party there is another, different party, a vertigo that she'll always want to feel more intensely. Sometimes the only way to feel alive is to fly too close to death.

'Yes, I am sad, sad as a circus-lioness. Sad as an eagle without wings, sad as a violin with only one string and that one broken, sad as a woman who is growing old. Sad, sad, sad … Or perhaps if I just said "merde" it would do as well.'[79] So I draw closer to death, play with fire, skate on thin ice, and put two pinches of salt in my soup. No matter how well I freeze time each morning before the mirror, a woman's body, Illouz reminds me, is 'a unit defined by chronology (and thus threatened by decay).'[80] Soon, I'll be too old to ever have kids. If only you knew, Revlon. I'm fucking fire and ice – or maybe I'm an eagle soaring high above it all, above everything, even its own extinction.

79. Jean Rhys, *Good Morning, Midnight* (New York: Pocket Penguins, 2016 [1939]), 34.

80. Eva Illouz, *Why Love Hurts*, 152.

Just because makeup can get us through the day doesn't mean it has any innate capacity for resilience. Rather, my eyeshadows are multi-faceted, a coat of many colours – paradoxical and elusive, capable of both oppression and deliverance. Indeed, for some people, even applying lipstick can function as a tangible act of resistance.

'Caring for myself is not self-indulgence, it is self-preservation, and that is an act of political warfare,'[81] wrote the African American poet Audre Lorde in 1988, then stricken with terminal cancer. Today, many a cosmetics company has transformed Lorde's radical quote into sales-pitch material, shearing its meaning from the contexts of her Blackness and queerness to sell us branded self-care in the form of creams, powders, and masks. I have certainly not been immune to this ploy myself – self-care has become a narrative that I document through selfies, casting myself in the lead role, my face smeared with expensive mud, cucumber slices over my eyes, 'taking care of myself.' Watch as the gesture of #self-care is converted into images, into products, and its inherent political dimension vanishes, carried somewhere far away on the ever-beating wings of capital.

As she wrote her famous line, Lorde wasn't thinking about the latest beauty trends – she was thinking about the nature of survival, of wanting to live, not just as a woman, but as a Black queer woman in a racist and homophobic society that would be only too happy to watch her die. Shortly after her diagnosis, Lorde's writings show her wavering between a denial and an acceptance of the horror of her fate. In her diary, she speculates as to whether she has liver cancer or not. Then, as if resigning herself to the prospect of her imminent death, she continues, 'Either way, I'm a hostage. So what's

81. Audre Lorde, *A Burst of Light and Other Essays* (Mineola: Ixia Press, 2017 [1988]), 130.

new?'[82] She knew all too well the ways in which the lives of Black and lesbian women were in danger, their premature deaths looming over them like the shadow of a colossal bear. The ways in which straight, white society tries and succeeds in erasing them, in invisibilizing them, removing them from the discussion, from the landscape, until even their actual deaths go unmourned.

A similar logic is at work in the fact that women of colour have long been overlooked by the cosmetics industry, and to this day, many still struggle to find products suited to their skin tones. It wasn't until Rihanna launched Fenty Beauty in 2017 that skin-tone inclusiveness became a major issue in the beauty world. The splash the brand made with its Pro Filt'r foundation, which was available in forty different shades, initiated a noticeable paradigm shift: it highlighted the sheer multiplicity of human skin tones and the marked shortcomings of the industry, which, in marketing products primarily for white customers year after year, had been reproducing the violence of erasure.

What Lorde meant with her quote was that, when you fight tooth and nail to survive in a system that would just as soon see you dead, you're doing something radical.[83] Self-care is political for some people precisely because they are not taken care of by society as a whole. As Sara Ahmed puts it, they find themselves 'not cared for, supported, [or] protected.'[84] They must constantly rage against a machine that seeks to swallow them, must sing survival songs to keep their spirits up, benefiting from the mnemonic qualities of repetition, the way it forces the body to remember not to let its guard down.

82. Ibid., 145.

83. Sara Ahmed, 'Selfcare as Warfare,' self-published: https://feministkilljoys.com/2014/08/25/selfcare-as-warfare, August 25, 2014.

84. Ibid.

I watch Gloria Gaynor sing 'I Will Survive' in a GIF, the silent looping of the lines like an unspoken chorus.

I've had the song on repeat for three days, drunk off the sweet taste of Gaynor's rage. I hear in her words the intensity of Lorde's desire to not go gently into that good night, but also a heart-rending howl that shook me to my core whenever I was in the throes of unrequited love for yet another guy who'd treated me and my friends no better than dogs. Bumbling guys all too happy to brush up against our pharmacy-enhanced pistils, but who, after they got the pollen they'd come for, wouldn't respond to a postcard or a text, would ghost us cold overnight. They ate us up, chewing with their mouths wide open. Maybe they thought we'd crumble; maybe they thought we'd lie down and die. This almost ritualistic form of dehumanizing behaviour started to seem normal to us, even natural. It makes you wonder if we weren't, through our love lives, engendering a programmed destruction of our collective psyches. I don't believe that 'what doesn't kill you makes you stronger' bullshit. To me, it feels like something you tell someone who's been abused or manipulated to convince them that it gets better, that their suffering really did have meaning, after all, that it was a springboard for growth. Rejection, heartache, and grief are one thing, but abuse, manipulation, and systemic violence have serious consequences that can last generations, rippling outward from their targets in ways both horrific and unpredictable. Me, I came out of my twenties humiliated and broken, almost lifeless. I'm no longer surprised not to feel anything. I don't belong to anyone – I feel no one's feet, or hands, or hair beneath my fingers. No one's but my own. It's fine, I think – I weigh less like this.

In my moodier moments, how many times have I daydreamed about reclaiming my body from the ones who've done it harm? While the song plays, I imagine what it would feel like to slam the door in all their idiotic faces. I was a girl who'd 'loved a man/with more hands than a parade of beggars' and now here I was, 'heart leaking something so strong/they can smell it in the street.'[85] I knew that feeling well. But I would survive without them.

I'm not the first woman to fantasize about a small measure of revenge, nor will I be the last. In high school, my English teacher told us that 'I Will Survive' was *the* song to rally all the women in the place to the dance floor, the one true jam to get any party going. As soon as they heard the opening chords, women of all kinds would take to the dance floor, ready to perform the choreography of their survival. And if Gaynor's disco anthem has the ring of triumph to it, it's because it makes clear that our capacity for love is intimately tied to our survival[86] – that as long as we know how to love, I know we'll stay alive. She's singing about a power that has nothing to do with control, nothing to do with destruction. It's power in its original form, derived from the Latin term *podere*,[87] which refers merely to the ability to do something. Maybe being able to love is the real power.

As much as it's a rallying call for lovelorn women, 'I Will Survive' – which was released in 1978, on the cusp of the horror of the eighties AIDS epidemic in America – also belongs to the LGBTQ+ community, a sort of quintessential gay anthem. Like other disco songs, it's helped generations of queer chosen families get through tough times, celebrating them with sass, with glitter and rhinestones, with their

85. Marty McConnell, 'Frida Kahlo to Marty McConnell,' self-published: https://martyoutloud.com/fridakahlotomartymcconnell, consulted April 23, 2020.

86. Nadine Hubbs, '"I Will Survive": Musical Mappings of Queer Social Space in a Disco Anthem,' *Popular Music*, vol. 26, no. 2 (May, 2007), 237.

87. Starhawk, *Dreaming the Dark* (Boston: Beacon Press, 1997), 3.

beautiful queer joie de vivre. Of course, I'd be remiss not to mention that disco, a genre born in New York City in queer Latin and African American clubs, was a music at the fringes of culture before being adopted by the mainstream. Disco is an art form for unity, a song for the survival of those who are being erased, even today, when the queer community still has to fight for recognition in so many different ways. In *Dreaming the Dark*, the American ecofeminist writer Starhawk says, 'The pain of all of us who are seen as the other [...] is not just the pain of direct discrimination, it is the pain of being negated again and again.'[88]

What 'I Will Survive' also says is that resistance begins to take root in bodies that the system tries to eliminate. Meaning, self-care requires not navel-gazing but a genuine return to the self. In taking care of ourselves, we might finally see ourselves through our own eyes, might watch our bodies appear to us suddenly, after all these years of being hidden. After all, it's only once you see your life for what it really is that you can truly begin to fight for it.

88. Ibid., 6.

In prison, putting on makeup becomes a humanizing ritual, in no small measure because the carceral system degrades people by robbing them of their individuality, confining them, rendering them nameless, and taking away both their ability and opportunities to show off. An inmate is a human being reduced to its basest state: an asexual body in an impersonal uniform, as if prisoners have been robbed of their rights to self-esteem and seductiveness. For women, prison sentences can pose a unique challenge, because life behind bars is rarely adapted to their needs, having been conceived and designed for male prisoners. For example, feminine hygiene products and cosmetics are often difficult to access. In 'What Beauty Is Like Behind Prison Bars,' a Refinery29 video exposé,[89] we learn that in the United States, some prisoners even offer sexual favours to their guards in exchange for things like tampons, coloured pencils (which they use for makeup), and lip gloss.

On YouTube, I learn about so-called 'jailhouse beauty' from a former inmate, Lizzie Kommes.[90] She describes the subversive tricks that women in county jails use to add a bit of dignity to their faces, using a handful of items that are easy to find on the inside: glossy magazine pages, sticks of deodorant, instant coffee, Vaseline, and Kool-Aid. Breaking periodically to admonish her cat, Velvet, a smiling Kommes addresses the camera, her audience. The bell on Velvet's collar tinkles in the background, and it's a reassuring noise, a reminder that Kommes is home, a reminder that the tricks she's teaching us about are bits of knowledge she won't have to use anymore. It's been a while, she says, but her body still

89. 'What Beauty Is Like Behind Prison Bars,' Refinery29: https://www.youtube.com/watch?v=Dp1DFvQTcJk, June 2, 2018.

90. Lizzie Kommes, *Jailhouse Makeup*: https://www.youtube.com/watch?v=ngZUTThsDns, March 22, 2019.

remembers how to do it all. She rubs the deodorant on the sumptuous crimson dress on a model in a magazine ad, and I watch as the white stick gradually absorbs the red pigment from the paper, watch her touch it to her eyelids. There's something almost awe-inspiring, watching her turn water into wine like this, creating eyeshadow whole cloth out of some glossy red paper and a stick of deodorant.

To make her mascara, Kommes uses instant coffee and vaseline, mixing them together with a little bit of water. Then it's her lips' turn: she smears them with the Kool-Aid, rubbing them together and then adding, 'The cool thing about this is that it tastes good, too.' Then: 'I think I coffeed my eyes, though.'

When you're fighting against a system that wants you dead, you have to be creative. Survival-life means having to make do with what you've got, so the ingenuity of inmates is nothing new. Deep in a digital archive, I come across a 1908 newspaper article[91] about women in a Milanese prison who licked and chewed the limestone from their cell walls in order to turn it into a white paste they could apply to their faces. Another one was able to turn a bit of red thread from her uniform into blush; yet another turned a window grille into a makeshift corset.

To punish the women for the sin of their inventiveness, the prison warden vowed to ensure they'd remain ugly. Those who abandoned their attempts at beautification could wear a fitted uniform, but those who kept on trying to make themselves up were forced to wear coarse and bulky dresses that resembled nothing so much as burlap potato sacks. It was an attempt to humiliate them by ridiculing their desires to be beautiful. The article notes that, within a few weeks, every inmate had miraculously fallen in line with official policy.

91. Author unknown, 'Vanity, Too, Laughs at Locksmiths,' *The Mitchell Capital*: https://chroniclingamerica.loc.gov/lccn/sn2001063112/1908-02-07/ed-1/seq-12, February 7, 1908.

In a society where we punish women for their sexual desire, wanting to be desired only compounds the original sin. Before it's seen by anyone else, however, makeup has its first effect on the wearer. When I make myself up, it's to make myself happy first and foremost, to turn myself on, to give myself the once-over. A woman enraptured by herself, even for five minutes in a barroom mirror, is a woman coming into her own power. She doesn't require anybody else's gaze to exist, and people – well, men – find that scary. They'd have us believe that this desire to be beautiful is pure vanity, that it's frivolous nonsense, or worse, that it's a kind of failing, a hole, something missing from the centre of a person. *Vanitas*, the Latin root of *vanity*, means emptiness, or nothingness, and aren't some women accused, like a vacuum, of trying to suck up everything in their paths? Such women must be feared, shunned, avoided – because if a woman who loves herself starts to seduce others, what's to stop her from becoming a veritable black hole of destruction? And so we seek to denigrate them, to degrade them. We claim that inside the empty shells of their bodies, there's nothingness, vacuum, void.

The newspaper article about the women locked up in prison in Milan reads like a sexist joke. But regardless of the truth of it, it does drive home a specific and pernicious gender stereotype: that women are creatures of the surface, fundamentally coquettish, superficial beings. To remain on the surface of things is to remain ignorant, unable to sink one's teeth into anything real, to dig down to the depths where life's essential truths are supposed to be hiding. So I touch down on the bottom with one foot, then push off, rise, and hoist myself up from the chlorinated turquoise shimmer of a summer afternoon.

The supposed superiority of the inner over the outer is just patriarchal ideology, yet another iteration of the false dichotomy of body and mind. In this school of thought, the body, which is material and profane, is nothing more than a crude husk for the spirit, which is intellectual and pure. It's an insidious mentality that runs like a dark vein through the whole of Western epistemology. Even Ferdinand de Saussure, the so-called father of modern linguistics, considered writing to be a poor substitute for speech, because the written word represented the externalization – and thus the deterioration – of an interior speech, one supposedly closer to a transcendental truth.

Sadly, the discourse around makeup replicates the hierarchy of this false dichotomy all too well. For instance, my favourite makeup artists all swear by something called 'glow' – that cool, wet, dewy, luminous look. Zineb Dryef, in *Le Monde,* writes: 'In recent years, it feels like the quest for an ideal complexion – a luminous, radiant reflection of our selves both in a physiological (I'm healthy!) and psychological (I'm full of zest, vitality, verve!) sense – seems to have gone global.'[92] By now, a jaw-dropping number of products on the market promise to give your face that very glow you're seeking. Yet the essence of glow is that it radiates outward from within – that your radiant complexion is evidence of a fire inside, less the result of a good highlighter than of a holistically healthy life. The goal isn't to find the right highlighter to apply to your skin, but to succeed in becoming that very highlight yourself – because the internal always feels truer and more meaningful than the external.

But what if the truth both enters in through our pores and exudes out from them? What if our deepest truths are visible on the surface of us, our skin hairy, pockmarked, and

92. Zineb Dryef, '"La beauté 'naturelle," signe extérieur de richesse,' *Le Monde*: https://www.lemonde.fr/m-le-mag/article/V2019/04/19/la-beaute-naturelle-signe-exterieur-de-richesse_5452583_4500055.html, April 19, 2019. Translation my own.

bruised? What if they sometimes take the form of the made-up skin of a beautiful ex-con, some ingenious plasterwork, a fleeting moment or two, cheeks so rosy they glow like fireflies, even when they've been condemned to rot for the rest of their lives in a cell? What if depth is, instead, a relationship with oneself, a desire to return to the self? And if that return to oneself isn't a question of inner or outer, but one of wholeness, of a beautiful, indivisible moment where the outside and the inside become one infinitely intertwined thing, two halves softly whispering to each other, 'It's going to be alright,' what then?

I watch the rays spill into my room, drops of liquid gold spreading across my floor. It's a perfect day to get nothing done, so I redo my eyeliner five times over. Montreal's in corona quarantine right now, so the only one who'll see my perfect makeup is the drugstore cashier. From behind a sheet of plexiglass, he asks whether I have a loyalty card. #çavaaller[93]

The sun hits my window at 2:00 p.m. sharp, pouring honeyed light into my living room. Everybody knows that the trick to taking good pictures is having the right lighting, and in this light, my eyes are green. It's a perfect day to take a selfie that'll force my L.A. sociologist to break his two years of silence. 'Oh hey, just saw your new profile pic. So good!' On SeekingArrangement, a man old enough to be my grandfather will think I'm 'gorgeous.' Another user, channelling Confucius, will say, 'It is not because there is a pandemic that we cannot be friends.'

Montreal is under lockdown, but my eyeliner still found a way to reach out and touch him.

I want money. Not money for makeup, but money to make things right. I've given so much through the years without getting anything in return. I was led to believe the exchanges would be sincere ones. But there was never any fair trade to be found. I fucked to be loved, wasn't loved, felt fucked. Now, if they want to stick it in my wounds, I'm going to make them pay for the bandages.

Because of the way the pandemic exacerbates class differences, juxtaposing the privileged with the vulnerable, the newspapers are saying that COVID-19 is eroding the very foundations of celebrity culture. While influencers are practised in the art of cultivating a feeling of artificial closeness, the crisis has forced the rest of us to contemplate more clearly

93. TRANS. NOTE: In Québec, many people started to use the idiom *ça va aller* to get through the pandemic – *it's going to be alright.*

the gulf that separates us from them. On Instagram, Kylie Jenner's baking a lemon cake, as if the apocalypse is just an incentive to get one's nest on. Her sister Kim, meanwhile, keeps bugging me to buy her underwear, while sending virtual kisses to nurses. Don't they work so hard? She's right: these days, hospital staff are no more than cannon fodder. Tasked with taking care of the sick without proper protective equipment, they fall prey to the virus, just as their patients had before them. But to call the cause of death 'coronavirus' elides the role that their working conditions played. Can you really call their dying a laudable sacrifice when it's really a massacre of state negligence?

While Madonna calls the virus the 'great social equalizer,' splashing about in a giant tub overflowing with rose petals, I'm stocking up on canned goods and rice. I think about riots, about rationing. Not all patients are created equal. Some don't even have access to a hospital bed to begin with. On Twitter, hashtags mentioning guillotines seem to be increasingly popular.[94] Now it's 'off with their heads' for anyone blithely saying, 'Let them eat lemon cake,' for anyone who wants us to believe in sincere exchanges based on mutual respect, anyone who tells us 'I love you all so, so much' on social platforms around the world – a love that comes with a product tie-in. It seems like only yesterday they were the vulnerable, relatable faces of the cosmetics industry. But today they seem like broken robots, skipping records, highway billboards in a post-apocalyptic movie. They haven't gotten the memo – maybe they don't watch the same news we do. On YouTube, makeup guru Tati Westbrook simply seems to have skipped over the pandemic entirely. Last I heard, she was listing off the best foundations of 2020, as if that was what we still expected of her.

94. Amanda Hess, 'Celebrity Culture Is Burning,' *New York Times*: https://www.nytimes.com/2020/03/30/arts/virus-celebrities.html, March 30, 2020.

My L.A. sociologist writes to me. The world is ending – it's a perfect day to ask how I'm doing. He tells me he's living in a yellow house on a California mountaintop, sends me a picture of hummingbirds drinking the nectar that he hangs from his windows. Reminds me to wash my hands. Tells me how much he likes my new profile pic.

Me, I don't have lemon cake, nor a yellow house – just two years of radio silence. I highlight myself, I contour myself.

And at two o'clock sharp, when the sunlight hits my face, I take a selfie.

Made-up.

I am not a robot. I'm not No Strings Attached, I'm not No Drama. I am the skin under the shiny eyeshadow, the girl I'm pointing at in my new profile pic. She's hoping that someday, someone will take care of her.

Ça va aller – but in the sea, it's another story. Due to global warming, jellyfish are proliferating far beyond the scope of typical jellyfish blooms, a phenomenon some are calling the jellification of the oceans. I read on Wikipedia that in 2009, a Japanese fishing boat capsized, pulled down by the sheer weight of all the jellyfish in its nets. Now, every day they're washing up en masse on the beaches of the world.

Jellyfish give me the creeps. Their bodies don't seem to have a clear inside or outside, don't seem to have surfaces, period. They're just clear gelatinous masses that reveal everything: the purplish blob of their organs, the yellowish lattice of their veins. It's almost indecent, isn't it, how frank they are about their fragility? They just love opening up, or maybe it's more than that – maybe all they are to begin with is openings, period. Couldn't they put a shirt on, I wonder, some underwear, a nightie? Honestly anything, as long as it covers up their gruesome animalness, the way they're all stomach, muscle, and genitals.

I want to take a branch and poke one that's washed up on a beach, to punish it for the sin of its overshare. *You need thicker skin*, I'd tell it, *and friends, and a face, or at least a mask.* The radical transparency of jellyfish makes me so uncomfortable – nauseated, even. Maybe Plato was right about the surface: it performs a necessary function, hiding from us the sheer fragility of life. The poet Lisa Robertson writes: 'Ornament is the decoration of mortality.'[95] Is that the grand illusion that we're trying to reproduce, the shameful lie of our carefully made-up surfaces? Our skin, our mismatched stockings, our heels, eyeliner, well-coiffed hair, and oh-so-rosy cheeks. Are we all just trying to hide the inevitability of our deaths from the world?

95. Lisa Robertson, *Occasional Work and Seven Walks from the Office for Soft Architecture* (Toronto: Coach House Books, 2011 [2003]), 111.

I want to stop being so distrustful of surface appearances, as if they were inherently deceptive, constructed only to hide what is true and unchanging in us. To stop seeing them as the curtains that go up before the movie starts. In fact, a screen is the absolute wrong way to think about them – so much more often, they function as liminal spaces between the self and the other, not used to veil or block off, but to feel, to touch, to let oneself be carried across the gap. Without our surfaces, how would we touch each other? Stroke each other? Hold each other? For that matter, how would we live? After all, it's the semi-permeable membranes of your cells that allow oxygen to travel through your body. In short, there's nothing superficial about the surface: it connects us to the world.

Since Greek antiquity, we've relegated women to the surface realm, telling and retelling stories that feature them as screens first and foremost, to the point of gendering the very notion of concealment. And so: women are deceptive. Practised in the art of subterfuge. Unholy. Snake charmers. Like that Japanese trawler, women cast a wide net and struggle with the weight of the clichés: cakeface, cum dumpster, airhead. They slut it up. When they glitter, they're not gold – they're knockoff bling, honey traps, eye candy. Something to be wary of.

In 2015, a meme called 'This is why you take her swimming on the first date' went viral. Typically, the statement accompanied a diptych: one picture of a woman all made-up, one picture of her au naturel, flaws and all. The implication being: in order to access a woman's real self, you have to catch her in a trap, force her to reveal herself. So you take her to the pool and let the water wash away her mask. Then, as if she were a beached jellyfish, you can pin her down and poke around in her fragility, her weakness, her ugliness, her acne and rosacea. Surprise! The perfect face she'd been trying to put on for us was an unattainable fiction the whole time. So kick the dumb bitch off her pedestal: it's time to pull back the curtain and put her back in her place, dig through her purple and yellow organs with a branch, and stick her nose in her own Jell-O.

This is what the Milanese prison warden was aiming at with his uniform trick. He didn't just want to punish the inmates but to humiliate them. Did you know that *humiliation* comes from the Latin word *humus* – black, loamy dirt, made up of decomposed organic matter? To humiliate someone is to bring them low, to throw them to the ground, to force them to crawl in the mud like a dog, to rub their face in it. He didn't just want to confiscate their makeshift beauty products; he wanted to confiscate their dignity.

Of course, erasing someone's potential to be an object of eroticization can also prevent them from being erotic subjects. The burlap sacks he made them wear turned them into a series of shapeless masses – levelling out curves and bellies, nipples and hips, reducing the body to a lump, its component parts indistinguishable. Faced with one of these, the gaze no longer even knows where to land, the eyes what to aim at, because a body so hidden no longer offers up a foothold – even for the person inside, who's been reduced to a confused mass that no longer recognizes itself, fuzzy, indistinct, form without form, body without body. But when we are desirable, are we not also desiring? In order to desire – to hope, to dream – you must first have a body. So the prison director wasn't just making the coquettish prisoners unattractive with his burlap sacks – in some sense, he was robbing them of their ability to want.

Desire is, broadly speaking, an appetite: a natural urge that neither begins nor ends with sexuality, one that cannot be confined to sexual attraction, regardless of the genders involved. Even when it is present in the body, that doesn't mean it's necessarily oriented toward the body of another. For that matter, some forms of desire have vanishingly little to do with genitalia at all. Despite what the neo-liberals want us to think, desire isn't even necessarily tied to pleasure, either. It might be more accurate to say that it's bittersweet, as the poet Anne Carson puts it. In her essay *Eros the Bittersweet*, Carson sees desire as akin to an attempt to pick a fruit from a tree's highest branch – it's a gesture that stretches out through time, without ever finding a resolution. 'The reach of desire is defined in action,'[96] she writes. It is movement without end. In his song 'La Quête,' Jacques Brel sings about seeking to reach *l'étoile inaccessible*, the unreachable star. But desire is not the star itself – it's the perpetual quest toward it. When we desire, we know, on some level, that our efforts are in vain. But who wants to wake from dreaming the impossible dream?

In a 1991 interview for the 'Angry Women' issue of *RE/Search* magazine, noted feminist bell hooks spoke enthusiastically about historian Eunice Lipton's proposition: why not write biographies from the point of view of what a person desired, rather than what they achieved? It's a decolonial way of looking at life and its value, emphasizing a person's inner truth and convictions, rather than what they were able to successfully grind out in a world that may have been working against them at every step. hooks remarks: 'Again, this goes away from the imperialist model where you're thinking of life in terms of "who or what you have conquered?" toward: "what have you actualized within yourself?"'[97] Which quests

96. Anne Carson, *Eros the Bittersweet* (Illinois: Dalkey Archive Press, 1998), 29.

97. bell hooks. *RE/Search*, Issue #13, 'Angry Women' (San Francisco: RE/Search Publications, 1991), 83.

did you dedicate yourself to, whether they kept you going or hastened your end – or both?

Desire is also something else – a sort of lust for life itself. Once, during my childhood, wanting to punish me, my mother grabbed a pair of kitchen scissors and cut a garish, asymmetrical swath through my hair. She wanted to humiliate me, to render me unwantable. But equally memorable is the aftermath: my sister and I in front of the bathroom mirror, crying and hugging each other, trying vainly to fix the mess with bobby pins. We were low, but she had not brought us down. There was nothing that could stopper up our desire to exist, our will to survive the forces trying to crush us.

The coquettishness of makeup is a form of resistance against the degradations of the world, the people and ideologies that would see us stripped of our humanity and turned into animals. It's a refusal of both humiliation and humility (that is, to be modest or lacklustre). Makeup exists to shine, to glow, to literally highlight the person wearing it. It elevates, celebrates, magnifies. You touch down on the deep blue background with one foot, then push off, rise, and burst through the surface. It's a moment in front of the mirror for you to catch your breath and breathe.

Of course, you might say, female inmates are no angels; they broke the law, and that's why they're paying off their so-called debts to society. But in this context, to condemn their coquettishness amounts to little more than criminalizing their survival, an idea Marlen Komar explores in her 2018 *Racked* article 'Why Makeup Matters to Women in Prison.'[98] And yes, it is a question of survival. Statistics show that most imprisoned women are survivors of physical or sexual violence. Often, they've escaped repeated, layered, and complex abusive situations that have left them weakened and incredibly vulnerable. Nearly 86 per cent of those locked up in women's prisons in America have reported experiencing sexual violence, and almost half of them show symptoms of post-traumatic stress disorder. In Québec, one in two women in prison has already been a victim of sexual abuse, while nearly seven in ten have experienced intimate partner violence. In Canada, Indigenous women – a particularly vulnerable portion of the population – represent a full quarter of incarcerated female offenders despite making up only 3 per cent of the women in the country – meaning they're overrepresented in prisons by a factor of nearly ten.[99] On top of these staggering statistics, many female inmates also suffer from mental health issues, the impacts of which are so often compounded in the prison environment, stressful and alienating as it is. These women have run the gauntlet of everything that's toxic in our society – poverty, patriarchy, racism, illness, and more – only to find themselves trapped within a system hell-bent on eating away every inch of dignity they have left, every last atom of pride.

98. Marlen Komar, 'Why Makeup Matters to Women in Prison,' *Racked*: https://www.racked.com/2018/1/3/16797784/makeup-prison, January 3, 2018.

99. Lise Giroux and Sylvie Frigon, *Profil correctionnel 2007–2008: Les femmes confiées aux Service correctionnels* (Québec: Services correctionnels, ministère de la Sécurité publique, 2011), 22.

I think of the women trapped in the Milanese prison, those badasses who chewed at their cell walls to be able to make themselves up with the very chalk holding them captive. Over a century ago, now. To them, wearing makeup was a gesture that transcended a self-love. According to activist Monica Cosby, a former inmate who spent twenty years behind bars in the state of Illinois, it's a question of autonomy, of power, of self-determination. Wearing makeup is a choice you make about your body – wearing makeup in prison is about taking back control of that choice. As Komar wrote, 'Having someone have that degree of control over you – deciding whether or not you can wear makeup – is a power dynamic of taking choice away, and it's abuse.'[100]

The carceral system is first and foremost an attempt to control the body. Humiliate, violate, put on a leash, rinse, repeat. It's an attempt to make the people on the inside shrink away like a *peau de chagrin*.[101] One day, all that'll be left of them is a docile carcass – enough skin to make a drum, or maybe a pair of shoes.

Cosby recounts the intense rage that ran through her during the guards' 'shakedowns,' their euphemism for group strip searches that would see forty to sixty women crammed into one room, forced to undress, bend over, and spread while the guards rummaged inside, looking for contraband. She would feel the anger welling up in her. Here she was, being accused of hiding things, as women so often are, being violated by a system, as women so often are. As she had been all her life. In an interview with the *Chicago Tribune*, she talks about the women still behind bars, *her girls*, her voice

100. Marlen Komar.

101. TRANS. NOTE: This is a reference to the 1831 novel *Le Peau de chagrin* by Honoré de Balzac. The title refers to a magical piece of leather that grants wishes – but shrinks every time it does so. Sort of *Dorian Gray* × 'Monkey's Paw' vibes.

catching.[102] Today, she's fighting for them, fighting to restore them their voices. And – as if to invoke a brighter future – she quotes Starhawk, one of her favourite authors: 'Somewhere a circle of hands will open to receive us, eyes will light up as we enter, voices will celebrate with us whenever we come into our own power.'[103]

I, too, would like to come into my own power. I, too, want a circle of hands to greet me, at least for a fleeting moment. In the mirror of a bar bathroom, underneath a Josée Yvon line, I'd like to come across myself and finally love her.

102. Annie Sweeney, 'Monica Cosby: "When All of Your Choices Are Bad, Then You Really Don't Have any … Freedom Is Having Good Choices,"' *Chicago Tribune*: https://www.chicagotribune.com/news/breaking/ct-met-women-prison-population-monica-cosby-20180717-story.html, July 18, 2018.

103. Starhawk, 153.

But let me come back to that colour for a moment, the greenish-greyish schmoney that keeps seeping its way into the makeup world. I'm not yet done sticking my nose into the foul, swampy greenness of it, easy as it is to hate. Maybe the reason American bills have been green since their inception is that their stagnant hue conveys a sort of stability, of sustainability, almost.[104] Does anything feel as reliable as that which does not change, that which is supposedly incorruptible? *In green we trust*, literally – because money has value only if we all agree to believe in it together. So if our neighbours to the south insist that their bills bear a timeless colour scheme and outdated graphics, it's just a physical representation of an ecology that strives to be immutable, as inflexible as death. Whether I'm doing my grocery shopping or browsing on Sephora, cash is my de facto religion, the only true constant in my young life, and I'm forever worried about not having enough. Yet its very abundance – never mind the *whys* and *hows* of its creation – is itself a form of violence. Whether a given fortune belongs to a stock-market financier or a medical specialist, the more wealth accumulates, the more poverty it creates.

Some days, the growing inequity that trickles down from rampant wealth accumulation seems like it's just part of the nature of things. Like a towel in an all-inclusive package, neatly folded up into the shape of a bird. The system behind it all articulates it with such grace that it seems normal to us, even inevitable. But who are the ones tasked with folding the towels, and who are the ones using them to wipe themselves off?

The repetitive, almost rhythmic, quality to the wealth gap also has a certain aesthetic value. It's a schism that, from some angles, can feel like a motif – the chorus of a pop song,

104. *99% Invisible* podcast, 'The Colour of Money,' Episode 54: https://99percentinvisible.org/episode/episode-54-the-colour-of-money, May 12, 2016.

or the pounding surf. Look, it's coming back around again. It reminds me of the black-and-white checkered floor in the entranceway of my great-uncle's nouveau riche mansion. As a child, I walked those tiles every New Year's, imagined myself playing chess on them, moving giant pawns. I wanted to be white, to take kings and queens, to swallow up everything, women and children first.

My great-uncle's fortune was made in plastics. Several years ago, facing stiff competition from Chinese firms, the business pivoted. These days, it manufactures individual yogurt containers, among other things.

As far back as I can remember, I, too, wanted to revel in all of my great-uncle's luxury, only without soaking up any of the violence of it. I wanted good vibes only, like you see in Instagram captions or Etsy coffee mugs: *Good vibes only!* Something like that, yeah. I wanted that part of the family to love me, and for that, I felt like I had to succeed in the realm of their black-and-white checkerboard pattern. But I didn't have the grace of my ballerina cousins, the crystalline laughter, or the grand piano. I smelled of old cigarettes, the ones my father chain-smoked. I was as chic as the inflatable mattress I'd been sleeping on. My tights had holes in them, and all my dresses were ugly. My great-aunt always wanted to know if the men I dated had good teeth, because dental health, socio-economic marker that it is, allows us to see into the future. But no. Will is a camera salesman, Bryan is a waiter in debt, and Noah drives a forklift.

When I was younger, I didn't think about all the coral reefs I'd end up ossifying into bone if I managed to achieve the success my family made me covet. I hadn't yet made the connection between my great-uncle and the disappearance of the reefs, those underwater wonders that are home to so many sea creatures, the aquatic miracles that give life its joie de vivre. I knew about money, but above all I knew its kind and human face, the one that brought me cocktails, gave me gifts, left little kisses on my cheeks. It was violence infused with kindness and good intentions.

More than once, I actually felt proud of all that plastic. I told myself there was a little bit of me inside every container my great-uncle's company produced. In retrospect, I was much more influential than I'd ever imagined, because my family helped create an island of refuse in the middle of the ocean: the Great Pacific Garbage Patch, a literal continent of plastic. Over the years, ocean currents have brought together tons of floating garbage, which now form an area of over 1.6 million square kilometres. I guess on my mom's side of the family, we don't just claim ownership over places, we create them from scratch.

And where would makeup be without plastic? Part of the beauty of cosmetics lies in its elaborate bottles, its ornate containers, its excessive packaging. Zippers and mirrors, ribbons and etchings, even magnetic clasps. Click. The mini luxury coffins where my magic potions lie in silence are complex things, typically made from a wide variety of materials, making recycling difficult if not impossible. So they'll end up in the global garbage heap, along with the other 120 billion units of packaging that the cosmetics industry produces each year.[105] Besides, it feels like everything I own is made of plastic: it's in my closets and chests of drawers, in my shampoo bottles, shower cap, and sponge, in my toothbrush. Cheap, lightweight, and pliable – you'd think it was the perfect material, really. As Roland Barthes said of it, 'More than a substance, plastic is the very idea of its infinite transformation. [It] is less a thing than the trace of a movement.'[106] Its inherent

105. According to a statistic put forth by Zero Waste Week 2018.

106. Roland Barthes, 'Plastic' in *Mythologies*, translated from the French by Annette Lavers (New York: Farrar, Straus & Giroux, 1972 [1957]), 97.

mobility embodies the very essence of globalization: the free flow of goods across the planet. But the way plastic moves is a morbid thing, a wholly lifeless kinetics. Inert, sterile matter – it's up to others to transport it, to ferry it around. It falls – or lets itself fall – where we leave it: in garbage dumps, in oceans, in graveyards meant for things that never really die. If the medium is the message, then plastic is a whisper in our eardrum about the inevitable end point of modern life: an apocalyptic wasteland where nothing grows.

Every time I walk into my bathroom, I find myself haunted by a photo I saw online once: a baby seahorse with its tail wrapped around a Q-tip. Of course, it's not just Q-tips that sleep with the fishes. The ocean is full of microplastics, particles some have taken to calling 'mermaid's tears.' It's easy to imagine the ocean crying, sobbing like a girl, its makeup all fucked up. The ocean falls asleep with its face all smeared, raccoon-eyed, as if she wanted to stain her pillow on purpose, at least so the sadness would leave a mark. And in this case, it does – these particular mermaid tears seep and flow everywhere, become encrusted on the rocks of shores all over the world, leaving them – like the ones on a beach in Madeira, Portugal – covered with an unearthly blue varnish, a sort of oceanic nail polish, a cling wrap of sadness. Scientists have dubbed it 'plasticrust.' It's a name that's almost comically vulgar – it reminds me of a Montreal punk band called the Vaginal Croutons, from an era when it was still edgy for a bunch of men to masquerade under a moniker exemplifying the hatred that we have for women's bodies. Because it's such a distinct kind of matter, plasticrust might serve to future geologists as a marker for the Anthropocene, the era marked by the impact of human activity. (À propos of nothing, *Miss Anthropocene* is also the title of Grimes's latest album at the time of this writing.) Plasticrust is mainly composed of polyethylene, a polymer found in most plastic packaging. So every time I order one of my little boxes to feel beautiful, I'm part of the plasticrust. Every time I put on makeup, I'm not just writing the story of my face, I'm also writing the story of human beings on the surface of the Earth, penning the same punk rock novel as everyone else: plasticrust. It's a story that begins as a poem, a poem that says welcome. Welcome to the Anthropocene! Where the seahorses dance with Q-tips.

Au revoir

Bienvenue[107]

107. Geneviève Desrosiers, 'Bienvenue,' *Nombreux seront nos ennemis* (Montreal: L'Oie de Cravan, 2011), 12.

There's nothing that capitalism doesn't touch. The title of the poem where Anne Boyer talks about the baby the pop star had with the billionaire's son – the little greenish-greyish wad of cash and guns – is 'No World But the World.' I found out Grimes was pregnant in a makeup tutorial on *Vogue*'s YouTube channel. I watched the video with the same fascination I reserve for all my night-time tutorial watching, like I was throwing back shots of some pinkish liqueur. But this one had a kind of uncanny quality to it. Grimes described her pregnant-woman beauty routine and ended up sketching black and red curls on her forehead, saying she was shooting for a 'pretty but ravaged by war' look.[108] There was something permeable to her, something porous. She might not have looked war-torn, but she definitely looked flawed. When she spoke about the damage she'd done to her hair with a series of home bleach jobs, it made me feel a bit better about my own hair – yellowed and dried out as it was after my own home-bleaching misadventures.

The gods of bleach are angry gods – quick to punish and slow to forgive. And I'd be lying if I said I didn't enjoy, on some level, watching YouTube videos of girls pulling out their hair in clumps, the BLEACH GONE WRONGs, and other hair disasters. There's always one pause that drags on a little bit too long, the tipping point where the girl in question gets a little too patient with the plastic bag still covering her hair. There's always the third consecutive dye job that doesn't land, the line that's crossed, that moment when she realizes she's flown too close to the sun and now her hair is done for. I'm not watching to laugh at her, really – more to accompany her through the horror of the journey, because I recognize my own all too well in it. It's a way to live out my

108. 'Grimes Pregnancy Skincare & Psychedelic Makeup Routine,' *Vogue*: https://www.youtube.com/watch?v=AwFl7J4LPdQ, February 4, 2020.

own heartbreak vicariously. I want to tell her that I, too, feel a fear in the pit of my stomach every time I mix the blue powder in with the peroxide.

It feels like watching Icarus plummet from the sky, intoxicated by the power of his waxen wings. He might not have been born able to fly, but he grabbed his fate by the horns and, using some rudimentary technology, baptized himself with the sky. In that sense, he's not so different from all the women who were born brunette or redhead but who, thanks to peroxide, ascend toward the sexual ideal that blondeness represents – at the risk of falling in the process. It seems like they, too, are the heroines in a kind of tragedy.

They're easy to laugh at, because they had the hubris to try to rise above their station, to become the other. Like makeup, bleach is an artifice that allows you to transform, to alter your identity. But attempting to make use of this forbidden power is a risky business. Changing one's identity throws a wrench in the order of things, because the construction of social ties depends on the stability of certain figures. By upsetting these ties, bleach subverts them. Blonde jokes – or any other form of humiliation that peroxidized women endure – stem in part from an attempt to restore social order. They're being punished for the freedom they've granted themselves, the audacity they've had in modifying and sexualizing their appearances. So if we're cruel to them, if we call them sluts, if we laugh while their locks burn off, so be it. This is what they were chasing after, anyway, isn't it? The act of 'dolling oneself up' is, literally, child's play. You can't be too surprised if you get made fun of.

Women like that almost seem like they can change shape at any moment, or melt away at the slightest touch, like snowflakes. They're so scary, we no longer know what they're really made of. But femme fatales are never what they seem to be, are they?[109] They're polymorphic monsters who defy description, upon whose selves no definition can find a foothold. As Derrida said, 'Monsters cannot be announced. One cannot say: "Here are our monsters," without immediately turning the monsters into pets.'[110] And sometimes these monsters are made-up, or tattooed, or bleached blonde. You can't pin them down like insects to add to your collection of beautiful dead butterflies. Their identities are fluid – they resist classification. They, of all people, understand best that, deep down, we never stop finding and losing ourselves.

I have an issue of this old feminist magazine from the nineties, a compendium of interviews with radical female artists called 'Angry Women.' In one interview, punk author Kathy Acker explores the distinction between people who, by altering their bodies, worship images – seeing in them an ideal that they feel compelled to achieve – and those who instead alter their bodies in order to actively seek out what kind of person they want to become, a quest for identity where they themselves are the star they're following. The latter are always looking, according to Acker. Looking for what, I'm not sure – Acker never seems to finish her sentences. But when we look longingly like that, isn't it because something is missing? 'When you look, you know you're "failing," you know you're inferior. You're inferior because you're looking.' Acker seems to know that it can feel like a form of inferiority to look *like* something without ever managing to embody it exactly. You know that you can never fully replicate the images you see – you can only look *like* them. So your quest must begin with an acknowledgement of failure.

109. Mary Ann Doane, 1.

110. Jacques Derrida, 'Some Statements and Truisms About Neologisms, Newisms, Postisms, Parasitisms, and Other Small Seisms,' in *The States of Theory*, ed. David Carroll (New York: Columbia University Press, 1990), 80.

On the next page, Acker talks about looking again, this time in a different context. But here, the interviewer insists on a more fleshed-out explanation: 'Looking for what?' Acker responds, 'Well, we're looking for a society that allows us the fullness of what it is to be a human[.]'[111] It's an interesting juxtaposition. When we modify our bodies, when we put on makeup, when we get tattoos, or brand-new dye jobs, maybe what we're really chasing is the possibility of a world that's not so cramped and restricted, one where we have a little more room to breathe.

111. Kathy Acker, *RE/Search*, Issue #13, 'Angry Women' (San Francisco: RE/Search Publications, 1991), 183–84.

Last week, while YouTube-bingeing a string of failed dye jobs, I watched a girl go through a genuine identity crisis. As her hair burned in her hands, she screamed that she was going to die, that she didn't understand her life anymore. It might sound silly to place so much importance on one's hair, but I get it. Our conceptions of femininity are inextricably interwoven with those of hair. In fact, in the Middle Ages, the punishment for female sex offenders was a forced public haircut.[112] Maybe we wanted to show them that they were nothing without hair, that their powers of seduction – their status as women, period – had been hanging by a thread this whole time. That may well be true, since culture so often reduces women to their bodies. Without their hair – their golden fleece – they'd no longer have either gender or sex. In the time of these spectacles of public shearing, society condemned their sexuality simply by revoking it, making them lose face by taking away a part of them. Whenever I dye my hair or get a drastic cut, it takes me days to feel like myself again.

There's a YouTube-famous hairstylist named Brad Mondo who's made reviewing hair disaster videos his trademark. He brings his expert perspective to each new Icarus, getting exasperated and making little biting remarks when he catches them being overconfident, but congratulating those who manage to stick the landing.

Hairdresser Reacts to People Bleaching Their Hair and Not Following Directions. Hairdresser Reacts to Worst Bleach Fail Ever. Hairdresser Reacts to Girls Trying to Balayage Their Own Hair. Hairdresser Reacts to TikTok Bleach Disasters.

In Mondo's eyes, home-bleaching is a self-evident mistake, roughly equivalent to drunk-texting your ex. Everyone knows

112. Roberta Milliken, *Ambiguous Locks* (Jefferson: McFarland & Company, 2012), 46.

how it's going to end, and everyone agrees you shouldn't do it to begin with. His shaming comments have a subtext to them, though: proper hair care is best left to the experts. It's a responsibility that's met via visits to the hairdresser, in creams and pomades, in treatments and oils. Necessarily, it's expensive. Mondo's vision has the advantage of turning physical beauty into a commodity. It's accessible – in a pull-yourself-up-by-your-bootstraps, plunk-your-money-down-and-take-it-home kind of way. But on top of his rhetoric, he's also deploying a sort of cosmetic slut-shaming, one where ugliness can begin to feel like a sin. For example, the error at the root of the bleach fail is one of negligence, maybe even one of excessive hubris. I can almost hear Mondo say, 'What did you expect, doing it yourself?' But if beauty really is a duty, then it's a responsibility only the most privileged can fulfill. Last time I got my hair bleached in a salon, it cost $800. That's when I decided to join SeekingArrangement. I felt an obligation to reimburse myself for the sex appeal I'd just purchased, that I had to make something of this hair that had now cost me so dearly. As I was trying to figure out how people could afford dye jobs this expensive, my hairdresser told me that many of her clients were sugar babies. From that moment on, it's been clear to me that beauty is more than just a duty or a responsibility – normative beauty is also a socio-economic marker.

But if Grimes is dating one of the richest men on Earth, why go to the trouble of bleaching her own hair? Is it an attempt to make herself seem normal to us, even humble? I think back to her tutorial, see her drawing her curls on, breaking every beauty tutorial commandment I've ever learned in one fell swoop. What a badass. I both love and hate her! But to whatever degree her dried-out, bleached-to-hell hair brings her closer down to my level, you have to be pretty fucking privileged to utter a line like 'I wanna look pretty but ravaged by war.'

The tabloids announce the arrival of her baby with Musk: X Æ A-12. What had begun as metaphor bloomed into reality – the wad of cash and guns was now a being of flesh and blood. The internet fills up with jokes about the newborn's unpronounceable name, a strange combination of numbers and letters, as impenetrable as a genuinely strong password. I think about what it's like to be a new mother, wonder if I'll ever have a child, whether I'll name her after a serial number. If I'll ever be pretty but ravaged by war.

Four days ago, I turned thirty. It was around this age that Grimes says she started taking care of her face – using serums, sunscreen, a jade roller. 'It's showbiz,' she says in her *Vogue* tutorial. Anyway, if stars aren't allowed to grow old, I wonder if we shouldn't replace 'war' with 'time.' Isn't it true that to age in a woman's body is to be ravaged, anyway? Pretty but ravaged by the years. Pretty but ravaged by capitalism. Pretty but ravaged by systemic oppression. Pretty but ravaged by income inequality.

Would it be possible to move through our lives pretty and not ravaged at all? Intact, untouched? Or, if devastation really is as inevitable as death and suffering, I'd rather be devastated not by a violence imposed on me but by one I've chosen for myself. In Québec, the term *ravage* also refers to a wildlife refuge–type space where deer can spend their winters in safety. Could I get a human ravage, too? A place that's open to the cold and the wind, but also to living things? And while we're at it, a scar for everything that ever made me feel like I existed, for all the winters I've journeyed through.

In an interview promoting her book *Stages*, American author Rachel Kauder Nalebuff imagines a future where we all care about the environment, where we all fight against global warming and economic disparity. Paradoxically, in this utopia, she believes that our grief will be even deeper, more intense than it is now. The devastation remains, she suggests – it's just the texture and intensity that change.

> I think we might even feel more sorrow, or at least feel it more deeply. It just won't be from structural oppression or financial precarity or climate crisis–induced trauma. But we'll feel heartbreak and disappointment, because [...] heartbreak is the other side of holding something dear. [...] And the more liberated we are and the more time and emotional support we have, the more we'll actually be able to feel the sorrows we carry.[113]

So maybe the real look I'm aiming for is: pretty but ravaged by love. I cried earlier. I don't know if it's because I'm thirty now or if it's the emptiness of my apartment or the Grimes songs I'm listening to, which are taking me back to a decade ago. Maybe it's the sociologist on the other side of the world writing to me from his yellow house, telling me that if I ever come to visit him, he'll help me dye my hair blonde. After that, he tells me, we can go for a walk in the mountains. Watch the sun go down together.

Colour flutters and flaps like a flag in the wind, a dripping, soaked-through, staining thing from which no one is exempt. There's no world but the world, and the one we live in is a cannibalistic system. Whether you're on a mountaintop or buried in the bowels of a mica mine, capitalism is an orgy of self-destruction completely in love with itself.

113. Rachel Kauder Nalebuff, 'What Does a Project about Death, Care Work, and Feelings Have to Do with the Green New Deal?,' *Thick Press*, https://thickpress.medium.com/what-does-a-project-about-death-care-work-and-feelings-have-to-do-with-the-green-new-deal-8166577f882d, February 11, 2020.

I want to return to colour in order to emphasize that makeup, despite its greenish-greyish tint, is neither good nor evil. It can only achieve meaning or political significance by virtue of its context; thus, its message is never the same. Makeup is changing, shifting, contradictory. But lest we forget, eyeshadows aren't the only ones in this position – so, too, are things like skirts and flowers, or, as Boyer enumerates them,

> flowers, flowers that might even be marigolds and petunias, perfume that smells like party girls, perfume that smells like dowagers, perfume that does not smell like flowers or more like flowers mixed with the urine of jungle animals and some tobacco smoke, perfume that does not smell like men, [...] the cracked dirty swimming pools of low-rent apartment complexes, bleach-haired boys smoking dope against the chain-link fence, the workers walking to their strip mall jobs, the strip malls, the dumpsters behind the strip malls, the karaoke nights in the bars in the strip malls [...] everything in the everything like 'there is no world but the world!'[114]

I'm trapped in the web of colour – the way it smears my whole being – but instead of questioning the oil-stain rainbows that schmoney draws and redraws on the asphalt of me, it's always easier to denounce it when we find it in others. It's easier to point the finger at people like Grimes, like my L.A. sociologist, or even institutions that like to wave their colours flagrantly – McDonald's, the Trump administration, Monsanto. Violence is so much easier to call out when it's external, when it's in the form of a convenient symbol.

Yet it's as uncatchable as the wind, and as omnipresent as the air. We breathe it in. We persist: violence is the Other. It's

114. Anne Boyer, 20.

the basic bitches sipping their pumpkin spice lattes every fall, blithely unaware that in the era of globalization, the very concept of 'pumpkin season' is no more than a marketing tactic now that industrial agriculture has erased the very principle of seasonal harvests. These days, you can buy pumpkin flesh year-round. Wake up and smell the coffee beans, basic bitches!

Fuck capitalism and, for that matter, fuck basic bitches. Fuck anyone who dolls themselves up with eyeshadows whose glitter had to pulled from the earth by thousands of exploited children. Let's spit on them, on their Lululemon leggings, their yoga mats, and their satin scrunchies. Let's exorcise our collective anguish by imprisoning them in gender stereotypes – provided that they're women and provided that their spending patterns are feminized (read: predictable, pedestrian, insipid).[115] Let's laugh at them suckling on the sweet nectar of a PSL, their grande Starbucks simulacrum, disconnected completely from reality, a disembodied voice yelling 'Pumpkin!' while serving up a tall cup of cinnamon, nutmeg, and cloves.[116] Let's be like my sociologist, horrified to discover that Grimes had fallen for a billionaire. Let's forget for a moment that there's no escape from the world we live in, that this world is, as Boyer reminds us, our only reality. If there's no world but the world, then this is the world I want to dream about.

115. Anne Helen Petersen, 'What We're Really Afraid of When We Call Someone "Basic,"' *BuzzFeed News*: https://www.buzzfeednews.com/article/annehelenpetersen/basic-class-anxiety, October 20, 2014.

116. Eugene Wolters, 'Understanding Jean Baudrillard with Pumpkin Spice Lattes,' *Critical Theory*: http://www.critical-theory.com/understanding-jean-baudrillard-with-pumpkin-spice-lattes/, September 24, 2014.

To live under capitalism is to participate in it. But we need to be careful not to normalize or essentialize things. It's not in Earth's nature to consume its own flesh. Or does it even have a nature? Can it be said to have any inherent guiding principles? Makeup certainly doesn't. Its capitalist, sexist, and normative tendencies aren't born – they're made.

While makeup has long been associated with anyone who's not a straight man, it's women in particular who form the typical target audience for cosmetics companies. But if all we see when someone says 'beauty culture' is a close-up on our decadence, we imprison makeup in a sexist world view that associates the ravages of capitalism with women, and, more specifically, with women taking care of their bodies. Of course makeup has a place in the economy. It is, moreover, a type of commodity that adapts particularly well to the recurring emergence of new marketing methods, like the ones driven by influencers. But makeup doesn't colour inside the lines – it's distinct, multi-faceted, and elusive. It's a product, sure, but it's also a cultural practice that takes up time and space. It's a series of gestures multiplied tenfold for each application, the repetition lending the steps a sort of mythic quality. It's my mother, reddening her lips behind the wheel, taking advantage of the bumper-to-bumper traffic on the bridge while driving me to school. The perfect redness of them, an O, suspended in time, a legend I memorized as a child.

To reduce makeup to the level of a pumpkin spice latte – to spit on the whole cultural practice of it as if makeup alone summed up the failures of our entire civilization – is a subtle means of gendering it. From there, you'd practically have to consider capitalism itself feminine, in a sort of neo-Genesis retelling of the sexist Garden of Eden story. Don't we castigate capitalism for the same sins we castigate femme fatales for? (Or women, period.) Using artifice and sex to excite, then sending the bewitched plunging into the abyss? Like a witch, capitalism is powerful, dangerous, and incapable of love, all too often dooming those under its spell to self-doubt and precarity. Its only moral code is selfishness and the fulfillment of its own desires. It's suicide, a poisoned apple, a bullet train to the apocalypse.

The perverse association between capitalism and femininity is nothing new – it runs rampant on the left. In 2001, the French collective Tiqqun published the philosophico-poetic work *Preliminary Materials for a Theory of the Young-Girl*, which posits the figure of the Young-Girl as the 'model citizen' of a commercial society. It's a circle jerk of philosophers and intellectuals attempting to anthropomorphize capital, while, at the same time, intellectualizing the abjection of the Young-Girl, all under the pretense that they're drafting the foundations of a 'theory.'

'The Young-Girl wears the mask of her face. The Young-Girl reduces all grandeur to the level of her ass.' Later, 'The Young-Girl's laughter rings with the desolation of nightclubs. The Young-Girl is the only insect that consents to the entomology of women's magazines.' And then, 'The Young-Girl's beauty is produced. She doesn't mind saying so: "Beauty doesn't fall from the sky," that is, it's the fruit of labor.'[117]

According to this boys' club of the French left, we might be better off conceiving of the economy not as a hydraulic machine but as a woman – she who is all of the world's ills, personified. The practice of casting women and girls as villainous is baked into the way we think, in particular through the metaphorical feminization of harmful natural phenomena: feminists in 1970 had to push to change the practice of giving

117. Tiqqun, *Preliminary Materials for a Theory of the Young-Girl*, translated from the French by Ariana Reines (Los Angeles: Semiotext(e), 2012 [2001]), 36, 37, 40, and 60.

exclusively female names to hurricanes in the Atlantic[118]; today, the Académie Française insists on calling it '*la* COVID-19,' even when all of French-speaking Europe has been calling it '*le* COVID-19.' Makeup is no exception to grammatical feminization, either. On YouTube, makeup gurus assign femininity to every product that passes through their hands, taking a page out of drag culture's lookbook.[119] Thus, whether they're being hyped or dragged, cosmetics are all *she* – even though English, unlike many others, is a language where nouns are gender-neutral. The result is an odd form of animism that reaffirms sexist stereotypes: women taking the form of inanimate objects that we're encouraged to or discouraged from buying. 'OMG she's expensive!' and 'Oh, she glows!' you might hear said of a certain pearly powder, as if they were haggling over a body or praising its attractiveness. Like women, the products are handled, undressed, shown off. It's only when the outer layers fall away that we can truly judge their performances, award them stars, recommend them to our friends. *Yes, she's worth the price; yes, she's worth the hype.* 'You won't be disappointed,' I want to mumble.

In this feminized context, makeup and capital go hand in hand. They look like Anastasia and Drizella, Cinderella's two horrible stepsisters. Ugly both inside and out, they have no choice but to resort to deception in order to seduce: they must butcher their feet, make themselves up, pretend to be something they're not. And how, if at all, could you separate

118. Unknown author, 'Metaphorical Gender in English: Feminine Boats, Masculine Tools and Neuter Animals', in *Druide*: https://www.druide.com/en/reports/metaphorical-gender-englishfeminine-boats-masculine-tools-and-neuter-animals, October 2017.

119. Giulia Zabbialini, '"Girl, we are serving looks!": the influence of drag queen's language on the "beauty gurus" channels on YouTube,' online: https://www.academia.edu/39236240/_Girl_we_are_serving_looks_the_influence_of_drag_queen_s_language_on_the_beauty_gurus_channels_on_YouTube, March 27, 2019.

these two 'Young-Girls'? How could you conceive of cosmetics outside of capitalism? In the media, the discourse around makeup frames it in strictly merchandise-oriented terms. And because cosmetics purchases don't meet any basic needs, they're perceived as irrational expenses, driven by emotions. It's capitalism in its purest form, at once excessive and unreasonable.

Strictly speaking, this view of cosmetics isn't wrong. For me, finding solace in makeup when I'm in pain is a tradition. I just got back from Pharmaprix, a MegaGlo highlighter in my bag. I just needed to feel *amazing* for a bit – *very blinding and very pigmented. Yes, I recommend this product and plzzzzzz, wet n wild, plz never, never discontinue this shade.* It would be so nice to have a powder I can count on, one genuinely safe bet in this fucked-up world. I want to be a star, fixed in the sky like a jewel, happy and at peace. Is that too much to ask for? Last night I told my L.A. sociologist just that. I said, 'I want you in my life.' And, 'I know everyone dies alone, but you're still going to need someone to hold your hand.' But he was just looking for a friend.

goodbye
never
impossible
shit
[...]
i am the little dog
searching for the milky way
my love said no[120]

He just wanted a girl to text with during the pandemic. He just wanted a girl who opens wide on occasion, a when-

120. Myriam Cliche, *Myriam et le loup* (Montreal: L'Oie de Cravan, 2005), 35 and 36. Translation my own.

the-going-gets-tough lover. He just wanted me in Precious Petals 321B highlighting powder, a pretty little flower who spends a month's rent on a plane ticket to go and get fucked – literally and figuratively. To get fucked in the wound I've had since the day we first met six years ago. *Mon amour*, I am never going to heal. In the meantime, I cover myself with various powders, safe in my conviction that I'm a precious petal with a serial number. I'm thirty years old, unique and the same as everybody else, made of nitride and dimeticone, not tested on animals.

Just now, my chest was so full of love it was threatening to overflow completely. A week ago, the sociologist told me to quit turning him into a character. I was on the verge of obeying him, too – I was going to delete him from the book entirely. But I can't help it! He plays his role so well. And I want to say to him, 'This is all I have left, *mon amour* – the power to sing of how you fucked my wounds.'

Makeup can be bought, unwrapped, gifted, thrown away. But it's always been more than just a powder in my purse. It's existed outside of monetized time – outside of Sephora, of Ulta, of Pharmacie Jean Coutu. Before it was bought and sold, it was hand-made. It's been used for purposes from the sacred and mystical to the purely utilitarian (for protection from the sun, for example). In fact, the first traces of makeup use might date back to over 100,000 years ago. In 2008, paleoanthropologists discovered traces of ochre pigment in South African caves, alongside tools they believe may have been instrumental in making it wearable.[121] Vestiges of a ferrous red-yellow liquid found in abalone shells suggest that our distant ancestors, too, were decorating their bodies. Even if we'll never know exactly when, where, or how ochre began to be used as an adornment, it precedes contemporary consumption patterns – and our very conceptions of beauty – by millennia.

It's easier for many people to view makeup through a much narrower lens, though, because it feeds into the idea that those who wear it are fundamentally frivolous, absorbed in their own image yet determined to attract those around them. An ethicist-philosopher I know once told me the Greek root of *cosmetic*, *kosmos*, referred to the stars – that's what we're trying to emulate with all our sparkling. We were on a radio show at the time, and it was a poetic enough interpretation that he saw fit to share it with the airwaves. But the Greek *kosmos* has less to do with the stars than with *the universe seen as a whole*.[122] It's a term that exists in opposition to *khaos*, the prelapsarian nothingness that it arrives to remedy by

121. Frédéric Lewino, 'Une trousse de maquillage de 100 000 ans,' in *Le Point*: https://www.lepoint.fr/science/une-trousse-de-maquillage-de-100-000-ans-13-10-2011-1384250_25.php, October 13, 2011.

122. Antidote, version 4.4.0, 2017, definition of the term 'cosmos' or 'Cosmos.' Translation my own.

evoking the creation of a new world's order. The cosmos is order brought to the primordial disorder, a story we tell ourselves to live. It's in this very cosmic orderliness that the Greeks perceived beauty. And isn't that what you do, when you make yourself up, or when you write your story down? You give yourself a beginning and an end. You're expressing your own cosmogony: *Once upon a time, I am that I am.*

Of course, the prehistoric pigment those researchers found in seashells, alongside other colours, must have played a role in the seductive games its wearers played, like the colours that animals brandish to stand out from their competition. The bronze-coloured clay must have been to these people what plumage and song are to birds: bodily markers in the pageantry of sexual competition. But to reduce makeup to seduction is to oversimplify it. Over the eons, people have also used ochre to write down their stories on skin. During rituals, it allowed for men and women from a given tribe to take on specific roles, to tell each other stories. By virtue of its appearance on the skin – which functions as a border demarcating us from a biological, psychological, and social point of view – makeup has played a part in forging the very concept of human identity.[123] When you alter your exterior, you're sending a message to those standing on its periphery. We need others – and they need us – in order to develop self-awareness, to learn who it is we really are. Moreover, makeup's earliest adopters, not yet having mirrors to sit in front of, could not envision themselves without imagining how they might look to others.[124] In painting your body, you're entering into a relationship with others – and by

123. Camilla Power, 'Cosmetics, Identity & Consciousness,' in *Journal of Consciousness Studies* 17, issue #7–8 (July 2010): 73–94. Available online: http://radicalanthropologygroup.org/sites/default/files/pdf/pubPower_JCS.pdf.

124. Ibid.

performing an idealized self for them, you're also revealing your desires, your aspirations, the person you dream of being.

It's a performance I always imagine to be as beautiful as the one my mother put on when she applied her lipstick in her yellow car. Every morning, caught in a traffic jam on the bridge, frustrated and angry, she took out her little red tube. As Camilla Power notes, 'In constructing her "fake" identity, representing her "self," not only does the cosmeticised performer ask "Who am I?" and "How do I look to the others?," but also asserts: "This is where I belong in the cosmos" in relation to those others.'[125] My mother was drawing the line between her woman's body and the girlish bodies of me and my sister, erecting herself into a summit that I promised myself I would one day scale. I used to dream of telling her, 'Look at my leather boots, Mom! Look at my car keys! I'm a woman now.'

When I was a child, this little ritual seemed to elevate her to the rank of adult. I was fascinated by her hasty performance of it, sometimes blended in with the little cries and shouts of road rage. I stared at her, trying to understand how the magic worked, that I might better replicate it. But my mother hated people looking at her, it drove her crazy. Did she know back then what it is that's scary about a pair of eyes scrutinizing us? The way judgment can fall like an axe, determining whether we pass or not. Because it's always the other that holds the power, the key to our identity. After all, it was my girlish eyes that had made her into an adult.

The first time she saw me in makeup, my mother laughed at me. She said I looked like a 'whore on Sainte-Catherine.' I was trying to be a woman, but she saw me as an impersonator. According to her, I was just playing dress-up, like a little boy who puts on a firefighter outfit, dreaming of being big

125. Ibid., 76–77

someday. The performance was a flop. My mother never seemed to miss an opportunity to castigate me for my attempts to explore what it meant to be a sexual being. She'd tell me over and over that I'd never be anything but a kid playing grown-up, no matter which lipstick or mascara I put on. So if I spent so much time trying to practise drawing a perfect eyeliner line, it was because I saw it as a way to legitimize my made-up face – as if mastering a technique then gave me permission to use it. To this day, I still use my expertise as a bulwark against any creeping feelings of impostor syndrome. I deserve my smoky eyes, I tell myself. I worked for them.

When my sister and I were teenagers, our mother would inspect our bodies each morning. With our arms in the air, hoping our tops were long enough to hide our midriffs, these daily humiliation sessions put us squarely back in our places: we were still little girls. It was like I didn't belong to myself – she still had complete control over me. One day, I asked her not to come into the bathroom when I was using it anymore. She told me that no child with barely three pubes to speak of was going to tell her what to do. I needed to get a lock.

Sometimes I feel like my mother denied me my sexuality because it threatened hers, because to her, seeing my body in full bloom was a reminder that hers was falling into disuse. When my twin sister got pregnant, my mother warned her: 'No one's ever going to call me Grandma.' In trying to prevent us from becoming women, was my mother trying to stem the generational tide? Maybe it was her own way of raging against the dying of the light.

Today, even with my eyeliner done perfectly, I still see a little girl in the mirror. I have my mom's words about my barely there pubic hair and my crooked makeup on repeat in my head. I watch as she cuts my hair, lifts up my shirt, throws herself at me. I watch as she opens the bathroom door, which

I can never keep closed. The anguish of her downfall flattens me like a house in a nuclear bomb test. I'm trying to keep secret the catastrophic truth I hold inside myself: I have become a woman.

So I put away my inner woman, like a beautiful, too-chic dress I don't want to ruin, and end up never wearing it. It's an overpriced silk number, yellow and teal, Miu Miu. But these days, the borders of my life are my apartment walls and bedsheets – there are never any opportunities to wear it. And, anyway, don't I prefer T-shirts and jeans? They don't threaten anyone; they don't sexualize me. I'm still afraid of upsetting my mother, of competing with her. So I put on a Hello Kitty act, taking a cue from my branded running shoes. Her voice rings out in red across my soles: 'Say hello when you see me.' A Grade 3 student who loves baking cookies and isn't much more than five apples tall, Hello Kitty never grows up. Instead, ever since 1974, she's occupied a liminal space between prepubescent child and sexually mature adult, the ambiguous no-man's-land immortalized in Britney Spears's 'Not a Girl, Not Yet a Woman.' Wouldn't it be nice to never leave this sacred in-between, to keep death at bay and remain cute forever? When you project yourself onto Hello Kitty you're not saying 'Hello,' you're saying 'Please, take care of me.'

And I do want to be taken care of. Is that a reasonable wish or just the childish whim of a girl who doesn't want to grow up? In return for all my sugaring off, I want money, sure – but most of all, I want to feel protected. I want to be X's wife. Y's bitch. Sometimes it's genuinely fun to play-act as a damsel in distress or a baby made of sugar. I told the daddies I spoke to that I needed their money to pay off some debt, or to get my driver's licence, to buy myself a set of appliances. But the real truth was I just needed it, period. I just *need* so much.

Please take care of me. One of my daddies picked me up in a convertible on my birthday, once. He'd gotten me a strawberry plant and a cake. When he asked me how much he owed me at the end of the night, I told him he didn't owe me anything. A strawberry plant, my birthday, some quality time? I realized that I was willing to give myself away for a strawberry plant. I know nobody's afraid of me – I'm like a pre-solved Rubik's Cube, all lined up already, no strings attached, easily understood. The real scary ones are the girls with desires. The ones who want to please themselves first and foremost. These girls make all the big strong daddies tremble with fear, because they're men who want so badly to retain a monopoly on that verb, *to desire*. It's because it's the verb by which we free ourselves, the verb by which we grow out of being a baby.

The company behind Hello Kitty says the reason she doesn't have a mouth is so people can project their emotions onto her. Personally, it feels a tiny bit BDSM to me, like she's being a little submissive, her absent mouth a metaphor for a ball gag. Because Hello Kitty isn't just cute, she's *kawaii*. This Japanese concept of kawaii – the etymological root of *kawaisō*, which means pitiful or pathetic[126] – refers to an extreme vulnerability, almost painful to behold. Things that are kawaii disarm us – they inspire us to be tender, to care for them. Like a goldfish I used to have whose bulging eyes seemed like they were begging to be burst, kawaii can, paradoxically, also nudge us toward sadism. Some days, you don't just want to cajole Hello Kitty – you also want to own her, to dominate her, to feed her a heaping knuckle sandwich.

We can conceive of kawaii as a way of seeing,[127] a means of perceiving the other as vulnerable. You forge an emotional

126. Christine Reiko Yano, 'Kitty at Home,' from *Pink Globalisation: Hello Kitty's Trek Across the Pacific* (Durham: Duke University Press, 2013), 54.

127. Ibid., 57.

bond with them, with feelings of tenderness and empathy, but an urge for destruction can also set in, like when you see a baby so cute that you want to eat it up. Besides, Kitty's vulnerability reminds me of the same trait in influencers – it's deliberately emphasized in order to elicit a specific emotional response. Vulnerability is at the heart of the intimate relationship woven between two parties: consumer and consumed, influencer and influencee, lover and beloved. We feel drawn to taking care of those who seem to need us most. 'I care for you,' I told the sociologist the last time we spoke. And when you care for someone, you're ready to give them your love, your time, and, above all, your attention – that valuable resource that influencers feed off.

So if I aspire to be a cutie, it's less out of a desire to be submissive than out of a desire to direct the way people look at me. It makes me feel like I have control over at least a fraction of my life, this YouTubing I do down the rivers of America, days at a time spent in bed typing 'best highlighter no cakey' and '90s vintage corset' and 'toner white hair' and 'olaplex dupe' into the search bar. Like a tired robot, I find myself clicking through different tops, looking for nothing. No matter how nice it is outside, so often all I want is just to keep clicking. *Suivant*, next. Maybe if I'm cute enough, my life will take on a whole new meaning. Ungaro Paris Style Shirt. Someone, somewhere, will want to take care of me. Flower Wrap Style size 6. I want to be a flower that doesn't exist anywhere else in the world, a baby luv, and live out my days on a tiny planet inhabited only by a little blonde prince in a cute green outfit.

The way we look plays a role in all our social relationships, not just the romantic ones. 'Me with a bare face and me with BB cream and filled-in eyebrows experience the world very differently,' writes Sam George-Allen. 'The beauty standard might be artificial, but its effects are profoundly real, and much further reaching than sexual attraction.'[128] Seduction isn't the only goal when you try to approximate a look – sometimes, you're just in search of material gain. Anna Sorokin, for example, a young con artist who posed as a wealthy heiress, hired a professional stylist whenever she had to appear in court, hoping to mesmerize the audience by means of frills, chokers, and baby-doll dresses. In fact, her lawyers were afraid a prison uniform would immediately incriminate her in the eyes of the jury. Her style matched her defence, and it functioned to solidify her arguments: if she had stolen money, she did it very politely, without hurting a fly. It's just that she wanted to start a business and needed a helping hand! I, too, could use a helping hand – so I invest my body, white, abled, and well-proportioned as it is. Before I signed up for SeekingArrangement, I'd never given a thought to its monetary value. Now I see the way my flabby arms hang and watch my value plummet. So I shave, I wax, I pluck my chin hairs. I play the game. And now I have a stove and a fridge. Thank you, daddy.

What goes up must come down; any image you create can be deconstructed. So, come evening, I dutifully remove my makeup. A Korean double cleanse erases every trace of the story I told, dilutes the text I watch disappear down the drain. Makeup-free, bare, imperfect skin is the cornerstone – the foundation – of most beauty tutorials on YouTube. Before the transformation can begin, the YouTuber must kick

128. Sam George-Allen, 'Where the Male Gaze Doesn't Go: On YouTube's Universe of Make-Up Tutorials,' *LitHub*: https://lithub.com/where-the-male-gaze-doesnt-go-on-youtubes-universe-of-make-up-tutorials, January 13, 2020.

off their metamorphosis with a clean slate. Because the narrative tension of the story being told depends on the breadth of the gap between the before pic and the after pic. For a story to be worth telling, there must be a marked difference between the two. As George-Allen explains, because the beauty tutorial opens on makeup-free, bare, imperfect skin, it helps debunk the myth of 'natural' beauty, the so-called intrinsic quality that brush strokes and creams can only hope to mimic.[129] Everyone on YouTube is acne-ridden, has an uneven skin tone, or redness – and no one says a word about it. It's like that poem we're all writing, that 'one true sentence' Hemingway's talking about in his advice in *A Moveable Feast* for how to defeat the blank page: 'All you have to do is write one true sentence. Write the truest sentence that you know.' The sentence we open with isn't ugliness, but the fundamental imperfection of every human being: there's a crack in every one.

The complex relationships makeup creates at times remind me of poetry's ability to do the very same. It's a text composed of unspoken words, a sort of embodied prose. You can write it according to the rules of metre and rhyme, or, as Rimbaud suggested, you can seek to grow and cultivate warts on your face. Through colour, the body speaks; it invites the other to read it. When I put on makeup, I'm telling the story of myself again and again. I blend myself in with a sponge, sweep myself up with a brush. I'm writing the story of myself, both the author and the text. It's a sort of bodily palimpsest, one that layers many gazes, many interpretations. At this crossroads of subjectivity, there is a self, taut between the poles of subject and object, a thousand miles from the simplicity of the Young-Girl that Tiqqun imagined.

129. Ibid.

The story of my skin requires the other's gaze – real or imagined – to come to life. It offers itself up, exposes itself. Anecdotally, the poet Paul Celan once claimed he saw no difference between a handshake and a poem, that both achieved the same thing. Poet Claudia Rankine expands on the idea: 'The handshake is our decided ritual of both asserting (I am here) and handing over (here) a self to another.' A poem, then, is the sign that says, 'Here.' I am here. But couldn't this definition of poetry also apply to makeup? It's a handshake – a 'conflation of the solidity of presence with the offering of this same presence.' And, as Rankine notes, 'perhaps [that] has everything to do with being alive.'[130]

130. Claudia Rankine, *Don't Let Me Be Lonely* (Minneapolis: Graywolf Press, 2004), 130.

There's no world but the world, and sometimes eye pencils write poems, too, pen soliloquies perfectly in tune with this fucked-up century. I've never seen anyone dip their fingers into a seashell in order to coat themselves with ochre before they perform a ritual dance in front of their family, but I have seen my mom coat her lips with red before she performs ritual tasks in front of her co-workers. I've seen people exchange gifts on Christmas and spend like mad on Black Friday. I've watched myself spending hours on YouTube, entranced by the glow of strangers telling me all about the things they've bought. Aren't these the constitutive rituals that create and hold up the capitalism under which we live?

My friend Julie tells me that what makes capitalism special is its incredible adaptability, that it's a shape-shifting mutant creature, capable of mimicking the cries of other animals to maximize its chances of survival. Yes, capitalism, like ritual, is changeable. It's an unstable hue, forever on the verge of a fresh shade, changing colours like a decaying organ. New bodies are constantly poking their heads up through its humus soil like flowers. It's a magical lamp that, when rubbed the right way, sprouts a genie capable of fulfilling our every wish. So as our desires change, so, too, does capitalism, mirroring them. When we want feminism, capitalism will drum some up for us. Do we want green, environmentally friendly products? It's got those, too, and self-care stuff, to boot. Capitalism is forever on trend, always offering us the right products to match our desires. When we want to buy things that feel real, capitalism will insist on the authenticity of what's for sale. In 2015, for example, in response to criticism from consumers disappointed not to find any 'real' pumpkin in their Pumpkin Spice Lattes, Starbucks added a tiny amount of pumpkin puree to the PSL. One pump of PR-friendly realness, please. From its official Twitter account, the drink crowed: 'In between a yoga retreat and a vision quest, I made a big decision to use real pumpkin. My dad is so proud.'[131]

In 2018, it was Lush's turn: the cosmetics company announced it would no longer use real mica in its products, so that its customers might shine without the taint of child exploitation ruining their looks. Instead, it announced, it would use something called 'synthetic fluorphlogopite.' The machine could continue to run, its conscience clear. With a move like this, Lush can keep the money coming in while remaining true to its so-called entrepreneurial values. But if we really wanted to keep minors out of the mica mines, we'd have to ensure, for example, that their parents were paid well enough to be able to send their children to school instead. To do that, we'd have to give up certain things – things like the economic enslavement of other countries. But capitalism isn't interested in making us give things up – instead, it wants us to play a game, a game where the goal is to avoid stepping on cracks in the sidewalk. As long as we can avoid those damn cracks, we'll be okay, everything's going to be all right, *ça va aller*. Schmoney makes the world go round.

131. Tweet by @TheRealPSL: https://twitter.com/TheRealPSL/status/633309027896700928?s=20, August 17, 2015.

It's New Year's Day. I've been in bed all day, working – I only went out to buy a cheap bottle of sparkling wine, something to drink with Kathy later when she comes over, arms full of seaweed and sushi. We'll watch some trashy reality show, laughing, pleasantly stoned off a weed gummy. Right now, though, I'm barely visible from beneath this avalanche of covers, and yet, despite being cloistered at home, I still found the time to draw on purple-and-gold cat eyes – a prayer recited in honour of all the things I don't yet know. When I brought my recycling down to the curb earlier, I remembered all the colours lighting up my face and blushed to my core. I was a priceless gem as I climbed up the fire escape, full of hope and intentionality. As I re-entered the kitchen, feeling blessed, each footstep on the linoleum was like walking on water.

'I am going to write fire until it comes out of my ears, my eyes, my noseholes – everywhere,' Audre Lorde wrote, when she knew her cancer was terminal. And: 'I'm going to go out like a fucking meteor!'[132] Tonight, I feel like a princess reigning over my own life. I'm not just surviving – I'm thriving. By celebrating myself, I'm celebrating the one thing in this life that's truly mine. Because I, too, want to write the story of my body.

When I make myself up, it's not that I'm unaware of how much money I'm spending on powders and creams. I feel the weight of the expense – both on my own shoulders and on the world, as the waste they produce spills out into it. On Reddit, I even found a spreadsheet that could calculate just how many years of eyeshadow I own.[133] It turns out that if I do my makeup seven days a week, using three colours a day, every day, the makeup in front of me will last at least six

132. Audre Lorde, 71.

133. Online: https://docs.google.com/spreadsheets/d/1xjC-d8WoV8PsvZwMUedSkU-PPRpXyvSfpeZK-Q29BpM/edit#gid=0, consulted May 22, 2020.

more years. Maybe I use so much because there's a hole in my heart, an emptiness the exact size and shape of a Ruby Woo lipstick.[134] I'm trying to fill this hole with a red MAC shade with bluish undertones that's pumped into the veins of the world at a speed of four tubes a minute.[135] I picture the bullet-shaped tubes piling up. Forming piles of ammo, tell-tale signs of a global forever war.

134. Tara-Michelle Ziniuk, 'Leftovers from My Cancelled Party,' from *Somewhere to Run From* (Toronto: Tightrope Books, 2009), 36.

135. Marlisse Cepeda, 'This Is the Best-Selling Lipstick Shade in the Country,' *Woman's Day*: https://www.womansday.com/style/beauty/a56758/best-selling-lipstick-in-the-world, November 4, 2016.

When I read about makeup, it's always framed as inherently frivolous. People are trying to sell me products, to let me know about the latest trends. *Graphic Eyeliner Is Here! Long Live Coral Red! Gloss Alert! Itsy-Bitsy Tiny Eyebrows!* Because it's feminine – or, rather, feminized – makeup is imprisoned in the world of merchandise, trapped forever in its plastic packaging. Which ignores the discourses on gender, identity, the environment, and popular culture all interwoven into the fabric of makeup – and it's only becoming more and more important. In 2019, the cosmetics industry was worth an estimated $445 billion; by 2024, it's expected to nearly double, to $800 billion.[136]

By then, maybe my compulsive, pearlescent body will be trembling from the stupid misery of all that I've imposed on it. All this overpriced garbage I bought. Who will I be then? Ruined, or disappeared? If I'm still alive, I know somehow, somewhere, I'll be made-up, writing down the story of my face, and my life. Making sure no one can erase me.

Because I still remember the sociologist's half-closed eyes the first time he slipped inside me. I watched him lose sight of me, so absorbed in his own pleasure he'd forgotten all about mine. The only pleasurable thing for me was the experience of becoming a scholar, because I was conducting a sociological experiment. I took notes, kept a log in my head of each of his grunts and moans. I got to analyze my own disappearance.

So if I'm writing down the story of myself today, it's only to make sure that I really did exist then.

136. 'Makeup Mayhem,' Season 1, Episode 1 of *Broken*, dir. Sarah Holm Johansen, Netflix, November 27, 2019.

Perhaps because it's so associated with falsehood, with mendacity, it's rare that we look to makeup to see how it might help us understand reality. In fact, it's capable of revealing much more than it conceals – within its layers it's possible to discern the inherent paradoxes of the twenty-first century. And while it does represent some form of language, the stories it tells shift and transmute, as does the world around us. To decode its many hues is to understand the society we live in.

Schmoney – the force that stimulates the accumulation of lipstick bullets – is pegged to shmoney – the bioluminescent currency of survival. When wealth stacks up, poverty deepens. Wherever you can hear the rustle of the greenbacks, you'll find people tiptoeing silently through the darkness, trying not to wake the giant shadow bear. Sometimes all it takes to save a life is a well-placed finger to the lips:

Shhh!

Schmoney or shmoney, take your pick – makeup flows in the veins of both incarnations of the term. It belongs to neither realm – or it belongs to both. While it augments my body and grants me the power to freeze time, it also plunges me into a death spiral of overconsumption. Like the Greek *pharmakon*, it's both the venom and the anti-venom, poisoning me and curing me at once.

For the philosophers of ancient Greece, cosmetics were seen as something to be wary of, quasi-toxic substances whose usage endangered their very conception of the world, since, as a vector of illusions, makeup was constantly threatening to blur the line between the real and the fake. It feels like all Western thought since has been tainted by this implicit disdain for materials (pigments, colours, ornamentation) that might somehow alter the appearance of the body. We've always sought to avoid these wretched things, these things that existed to replicate or dissimulate reality. But, as Lichtenstein writes, 'the aim of this distinction is to save the identity of reality from any possible confusion that might damage the dignity of whoever relies on it.'[137] It was to solidify his vision of the world that Plato placed cosmetics in opposition to a so-called universal and immutable reality. Because anything capable of transforming something is proof of the world's inherent changeability. Nothing is immutable. From this perspective, the world is at the mercy of our every gesture, even one so simple as applying a primer. And if cosmetics are scary, those who claim the transformative power they hold as a right are doubly so. They embody the movement and instability inherent to the concept of identity. That's why we don't just look down our noses at makeup, but also at those who wear it.

I scroll through my old selfies, swiping right to move backwards in time. My face is a projection screen on which the drama of all my encounters, my stories of love and friendship, is played out. A border is also an opening, and it's true for me, too. 'This is the pharmakon: An indiscrete threshold where our bodies exchange information with an environment.'[138] Here I am, at the lip of the threshold, with my hairs and my blackheads, my nascent wrinkles and my reddened eyelids.

Last night, a paranoid thought overtook me. I began to wonder if the sociologist had ever really existed. I worried that maybe I'd dreamt him up. Maybe I was going mad. Wasn't he the perfect bird whose arrival I'd waited for for six long years? Wasn't I ready for us to spend the end of the world together? And still he'd said no. And still he'd added: *but if you ever want a friend to play with, you know where to find me.*

137. Jacqueline Lichtenstein, my translation, 170.

138, Lisa Robertson, 'How to Colour,' *Occasional Work and Seven Walks from the Office for Soft Architecture* (Toronto: Coach House Books, 2011 [2003]), 123.

No drama.

No strings attached.

I spent the whole night recording myself, filming myself, documenting the existence of this man I had loved, touched, kissed – with whom I'd scaled mountains and crossed deserts. I even googled his name, just to make sure I hadn't imagined him. Maybe that's why I'm always writing down the story of myself, studying my face in the bathroom mirror for hours at a time. I want to exist, at least in my own eyes. I want to believe in myself.

One time, I'd told him: I like the little brown spot you have on one of your eyelids. But he didn't know what I was talking about, because he hated looking at himself in the mirror. Behind those closed-tight lids was the whole of Western philosophy's wariness of anyone who might stare too long at their own reflection. When I think back on that moment, I wonder if his discomfort with mirrors didn't have something to do with a fear of what, exactly, he might see in them.

Me, I like to look at myself. I let the mirror multiply me – it's a form of play. Makeup redraws the map of my face, hardening here, softening there, colouring in all over. Straight lines are right out. My bathroom is the kingdom of the diffuse, the muted, the oblique, the zig-zagging. It's my party and I'll cry raccoon-eye tears if I want to. Every day, I leave pieces of me behind – bits of colour, dead birds. Lichtenstein again: 'Unlike the line, which is already the result of a course taken and the start of a drawing, color is not the beginning of a figure.'[139] When it speaks, it's in a language that sounds new; when it writes, it uses unfamiliar characters. But, like the ever-changing world, it's telling a story of life – and also one of death. Doesn't the colour of skin change when the blood beneath the surface stops flowing?

139. Jacqueline Lichtenstein, 51.

For Lisa Robertson, colours – flowing and smudgeable, with their murky relationships to boundaries – are capable of inciting political change: 'Dangerously pigment smears. Artifice is the disrespect of the propriety of borders.'[140] I feel like I'm doing the same thing when I write: I stretch out, drool a little, quietly rearrange the lines that form the skeleton of the narrative, taking back the reins of the story.

If we rarely interrogate cosmetics in any meaningful sense – if we relegate them to the realm of 'women's issues,' chick lit for reality – perhaps it's because they threaten the great chain of being, a hierarchy we want to remain untouched. Makeup is brash, and loud. It mars and moistens the skin by turn. Seduces. It whispers metamorphosis and change. And it's in this change that there lies hope. Isn't it always change that the crowd is calling for, in riots and in demonstrations? Flouting the rules and revelling in their disobedience.

140. Lisa Robertson, 123.

It's late, so I take my makeup off. Command-Z to undo. Watch the lines of colour streaming down into the sink. Every day, in front of my bathroom mirror, I'm practising the steps of the great journey into the wild we'll all take eventually. I'm slowly learning how to die.

I wanted this to be a book about makeup. Part essay, part investigation, part research, part exploration. I wanted to meditate on this thing that colours all my sleepless nights. And yet it seems like there's a broken heart forever on the tip of my tongue, forever at the nib of my pen. Because here I am, talking about love again.

Someone once asked me whether I thought the fact that love made its way into all my books was good news. But love is neither good news nor bad news. In truth, it's not news at all, although it does constantly require new forms of expressing itself. Like death, it's at the very heart of the human condition.

N.,
You were the person I wanted to take care of.
We all need someone to hold our hand when we die, even if we die alone.
That's all.
I'm sad but I'm also relieved. I've suffered a lot.

For a long time, it seemed like I was turning in circles, a single 'I' lodged in my throat, an 'I' that never stepped outside of itself, an 'I' that couldn't stop scrutinizing itself in the bathroom mirror, an 'I' that blew through money at Jean Coutu buying frivolous things, hair masks and shiny barrettes.

So often people have told me, 'Daphné, we're tired of hearing the same old stories of heartache and heartbreak. Get a brush and dustpan and sweep the shards of all this teenage crap up off the floor. Don't tell us you're going to keep spouting the same stories over and over again?'

But I'm not going to apologize. Because, like bleach and makeup, like fear and death, love teaches us what you need in order to transform: a wound.

That's all, *mon amour*, that's all.

ABOUT THE AUTHOR AND TRANSLATOR

Poet and literary translator **Daphné B.** lives and works in Montreal. She spends a lot of time reading, writing, and watching videos on YouTube. She published *Bluetiful* in 2015 (Les Éditions de l'Écrou), then *Delete* (L'Oie de Cravan) in 2017, in addition to writing in numerous magazines including *Nouveau Projet*, *Liberté*, *Vice*, *Spirale*, *Zinc*, and *Estuaire*. She co-founded the feminist platform Filles Missiles and is a regular contributor to the radio show *Plus on est de fous, plus on lit*, on Radio-Canada.

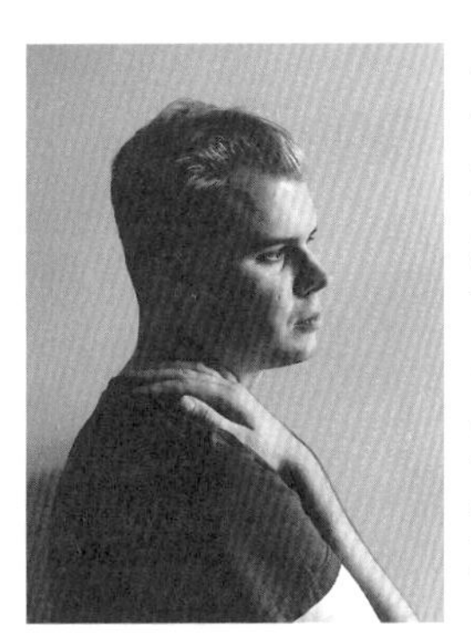

Alex Manley is a Montreal/Tiohtià:ke writer and editor whose work has been published by *Maisonneuve* magazine, *Hazlitt*, *The Walrus*, *Grain*, *Vallum*, and the *Literary Review of Canada*, among others. Their debut poetry collection, *We Are All Just Animals & Plants*, was published by Metatron Press in 2016.

Typeset in Albertina and Futura.

Printed at the Coach House on bpNichol Lane in Toronto, Ontario, on Lynx Cream paper. This book was printed with vegetable-based ink on a 1973 Heidelberg KORD offset litho press. Its pages were folded on a Baumfolder, gathered by hand, bound on a Sulby Auto-Minabinda, and trimmed on a Polar single-knife cutter.

Coach House is located on the traditional territory of many nations, including the Mississaugas of the Credit, the Anishnaabeg, the Haudenosaunee, the Chippewa, and the Wendat peoples, and is now home to many diverse First Nations, Métis, and Inuit people. Toronto is covered by Treaty 13 signed with the Mississaugas of the Credit, and the Williams Treaties signed with multiple Mississaugas and Chippewa bands. We are grateful to live and work on this land.

Edited by Alana Wilcox
Cover art *A Woman Relinquishing Her Power in Exchange for Unlimited Data* by Lola Rose Thompson, Instagram: @lolarosethompson
Cover and interior design by Crystal Sikma
Author photo by JF Lemire
Translator photo by Blair Elliott

Coach House Books
80 bpNichol Lane
Toronto ON M5S 3J4
Canada

416 979 2217
800 367 6360

mail@chbooks.com
www.chbooks.com